RALP

SIR HENRY COOPER

A BOXING KNIGHT

CANDY JAR BOOKS · CARDIFF
2025

Editor: Terry Cooper
Editorial: Shaun Russell & Keren Williams

All images are provided by Derek Rowe, with
the exception of the single colour photo of Henry (Philip
Sharkey) and Henry and Ralph (Ralph Oates)

Printed and bound in the UK by
4edge, 22 Eldon Way, Hockley, Essex, SS5 4AD

ISBN: 978-1-918097-01-6

Published by
Candy Jar Books
Mackintosh House
136 Newport Road, Cardiff, CF24 1DJ
www.candyjarbooks.co.uk

This book is dedicated to Ruby Oates,
who was a very special lady.

Foreword

I was pleased to write the introduction for Ralph Oates' latest book, *Sir Henry Cooper: A Boxing Knight.* This publication covers each one of Henry's professional fights in great detail. Much research has clearly been done in compiling the book. I believe boxing enthusiasts will find it a very interesting read. Henry had an exceptional career: he not only won a number of titles in the ring – these being the British, European and Commonwealth – but also the hearts of many who followed the sport.

Boxing is a hard sport, and it often tests the character of the participants in the ring who may suffer setbacks during the duration of their careers. Henry had his share of setbacks and showed that he had the fighting heart to come back and succeed. Of course, the world heavyweight crown eluded him during his career.

However, when you consider that the man at the top at

that particular time was none other than the great Muhammad Ali, you can understand why the title was out of his reach.

To his credit, Henry did tackle Ali on two occasions. He may have lost, but he did so with credit (you can read about his encounters with Ali inside this book). I met Henry a number of times over the years at various functions, and apart from boxing, we both had a passion for golf.

You could say that after our time in boxing was over, we went from rounds of boxing to playing rounds of golf, and hitting a ball rather than an opponent – the advantage here being that the ball does not hit back, which is a big plus.

So step back in time and appreciate the career of Sir Henry Cooper when turning the pages of this book.

Jim Watt, MBE
Former WBC World, European and British Lightweight Champion

About the Author

Ralph Oates, a former amateur boxer, has been writing about the sport for over twenty-seven years. In that time, he has written thirteen books on boxing. He contributed to *The British Boxing Board of Control Yearbook* – the leading book of its kind for eighteen years. Ralph has also contributed to the magazines *My Planet Liverpool* and *Beyond* and to *The British Boxing Journal.* He has had his own boxing column in the *Essex Courier*, the monthly paper, *Take One*, and monthly magazine *Bounce.* At present, Ralph writes a boxing column for the *Cardiff Times.* He is also a former boxing consultant for Guinness World Records and has complied boxing questions for the national TV show *Who Dares Wins.*

Ringside Charitable Trust

Ralph Oates is donating his royalties from the sale of this book to the Ringside Charitable Trust. The aim of this charity is to provide a residential home for ex-boxers to be cared for when they encounter various difficulties after they retire from the sport.

Acknowledgements

In putting this book together, I would like to thank my brother, Howard Oates, for his assistance in checking this publication. This is by no means an easy task. Also, thanks to my sister-in law, Denise Oates, for her technical advice, which was vital during the project.

Further thanks must also go to the two excellent photographers who contributed the images for the book: Derek Rowe and Philip Sharkey – two men who are the best in their field, constantly producing top-quality images.

Also, I would like to thank my publisher, Shaun Russell, for his support and encouragement while writing this book.

May I also extend my thanks to former WBC World Lightweight, British and European champion, Jim Watt MBE, for taking the time to write the foreword for the book. Jim was an outstanding boxer whose professional resumé comprised of forty-six bouts, winning thirty-eight, and losing eight. He has been a credit to boxing, both inside and outside of the ring.

Professional Boxing Organisations

WBA	World Boxing Association
WBC	World Boxing Council
WBO	World Boxing Organisations
IBF	International Boxing Federation
WBF	World Boxing Federation
NBA	National Boxing Association

Amateur Boxing Organisations

ABA Amateur Boxing Association

Introduction

There was a time when it seemed that British heavyweight boxing just didn't have the quality of fighter in its midst to acquire the world championship. True, the UK produced some pretty decent boxers at the weight, some of whom were the best in Europe, often confirming that fact by winning the continental crown, and while that is a big chunk of territory to be champion of, it was not the world crown.

The various Brits who did fight their way to contender status to earn a crack at global honours would fail when coming up against the defending title holder, who would prove to be a superior ring artist, and hence suffer the consequences of an overwhelming defeat. To their credit, the fighters from Britain bravely performed, but bravery alone does not put a contender on the championship throne.

The Americans ruled the roost. The fighters from the USA were kings of the hill, a league above the rest on the planet – that was an indisputable fact. If the title changed hands, it would pass to yet another American, such was their dominance of the division.

True, there was the odd exception when a champion from the USA lost the title to a fighter from outside of America, but the crown soon returned to the States. The nation appeared to produce one top heavyweight after another on what seemed like a conveyor belt system. It was, of course, not just the British who failed to annex the championship, but fighters from other parts of the world who would be defeated when going for that elusive and most prized crown.

Make no mistake – the Heavyweight Championship is a prized crown. It's a title which captivates the fans of the sport and attracts the media more than any other weight division, with perhaps a few exceptions. It is the banner weight division in boxing. Winning the championship leads the holder to big-money fights, ensuring that his bank balance is more than a little healthy. True greats in the division like Jack Johnson, Jack Dempsey, Gene Tunney, Joe Louis, Rocky Marciano, Muhammad Ali, Joe Frazier, Larry Holmes and George Foreman, all from the USA, were light years ahead of the European fighters around at that time.

The UK eventually had a slight ray of hope in a fighter named Henry Cooper: it was hoped that he might be able to balance the scales and break the hold of the Americans, and win the world crown. Cooper did not, in fact, earn the status of World Heavyweight Champion. Nevertheless, he became a hero, a man of both dignity and honour. The fighter was affectionately known to the public as 'Our 'Enry', a boxer who was much respected by fans and opponents alike. Cooper brought a great deal of excitement to the sport during his boxing career.

His popularity was such that it extended way beyond the prize ring. He was able to connect with people with his down-to-earth and friendly manner, which endeared him to many. Even non-boxing fans knew of him – those who didn't care much for boxing would always show interest whenever news of a Cooper fight was announced. He was a man of the people, always approachable, always having time to listen to the fans whenever they spoke to him.

Cooper was immediately liked by those who came into contact with him. He was a true national treasure, of that there is no doubt. He was a family man, which also resonated well with the public at large. Cooper was a class act, who represented all that was good in boxing. His left hook, known as 'Enry's 'Ammer', was a potent punch, feared by many who opposed Cooper in the ring, and for good reason.

Once it found its target, the fight was over. Cooper was a good technical boxer. His one weakness was being prone to eye cuts, which often put him at a disadvantage when fighting. He suffered his share of setbacks, the kind of which would have made many other fighters think about finding another career. Not Cooper.

He overcame the setbacks, showing heart and determination in doing so. He was every inch a fighter. It should be remembered that Cooper fought in an era when the USA maintained its hold on the heavyweight crown. Boxers like Floyd Patterson, Sonny Liston, Muhammad Ali, Ernie Terrell, Jimmy Ellis and Joe Frazier all held the title at one time or another. Now that is a tough lineup.

There were no easy pickings there for the British boxer. The world's top ten was full of fighters from the United States who were dangerous. There was no let-up with the grip the USA had on the heavyweight division. They bossed the division. They were leagues above the rest. Whenever a boxer from outside of the States challenged for the crown, you always knew deep down that he would lose in his bid, and the crown would stay in American hands.

The last British-born world heavyweight king at that time was Bob Fitzsimmons. He ruled from 1897-1899. It had to be wondered if Britain would ever produce another man like Fitzsimmons, who was capable of bringing the much sought-after title back to Britain.

Cooper made an impact on 18th June 1963, when he fought the undefeated Muhammad Ali – then 'Cassius Clay'– flooring him for a count in round four. Clay got up and won the contest, stopping Cooper in the following round.

Nevertheless, the flooring of Clay by Cooper made the news big time, giving the British heavyweight division a mark of respect. The film clip has been shown many times over the years on TV and various other news outlets around the globe. At that moment, Cooper became an international name, a man who had something to offer, and someone who just might shake things up a little in the heavyweight poundage

During his time in the professional ring, Cooper did not venture to the USA to box. That was prudent in many ways, since the land of the stars and stripes was a tough place for any non-American heavyweights to compete in. Even the lower-ranked boxers in the states were often a handful to share the ring with. That says it all.

Cooper had just one crack at the title during his career, and that was a return contest against Muhammad Ali, who was now the reigning WBC world heavyweight champion in a bout which took place on 21st May, 1966. On the night, Ali was on his game – a master of his craft, a man who looked – and was – unbeatable. The end for Coopr came in round six, when he once again sustained a badly cut left eye. The British fighter, without doubt, shed more than his share of blood when boxing in the ring.

Over the years, there have been a number of outstanding world heavyweight kings who have thrilled the fans with their performances. However, many historians consider Ali to be the greatest heavyweight world champion of them all. They back up their findings with solid facts, which are difficult to argue with when examined closely. So the loss to such a man as Ali was hardly a disgrace, but it was still disappointing that Cooper was unable to reach the very top and claim the supreme title in boxing. Even holding the title for a short time would have been a big achievement for the British fighter.

Sadly, it was not to be. It was clear that Ali and Cooper had a great deal of respect and admiration for each other. They remained friends long after their fighting days were over. In conversation, Ali often recalled the occasion when Cooper's famed left hook put him on the canvas and almost altered the course of boxing history.

Despite not winning the world title during his time in boxing, Cooper achieved so much. He went on to make history on his own account. He became the first boxer to win three Lonsdale belts outright, which is a remarkable achievement, became the longest reigning British heavyweight champion, and the first to win the European (EBU) title on three separate occasions. Cooper also received a knighthood, which was a fantastic honour for both him and the sport in general. This revealed just how highly Cooper was thought of in the UK.

After Cooper retired from the ring, he was in great demand, appearing in a wide range of TV shows and advertisements for certain products, which felt the advantage of having the Cooper brand associated with their product. Such was his immense pulling power. It was truly amazing how well he was liked.

Winning the world heavyweight crown would have been fantastic – a life-changing experience for Cooper. However, even while not holding the crown, he had an excellent career, one which he could look back on with pride. Many a boxer who's laced on a pair of gloves would have liked to have received the kind of acclaim Cooper had during his stint in the ring. His name was synonymous with British heavyweight boxing. He was the main man in the domestic division. He was an icon – a man who was greeted with enthusiasm by fans wherever he went. Cooper was one of their own, a man many could identify with.

It was my great pleasure to have met Henry at a boxing function some years ago. It was a great moment for me, since I was meeting someone very special. Here was a man whom I had watched many times in action from afar, and now I was face-to-face with him. It didn't take long to understand why he was so very popular with people of all standing. He was charming in every way. We spoke at length about boxing, and, of course, the left hook which famously put Ali on the deck during their first encounter.

Everyone wanted to speak to Henry and shake his hand. He hardly had a moment to himself all evening, such was his popularity. The term 'legend' is often overused today when praising certain individuals in various sports. Not in the case of Cooper. He became a true legend, and in so doing, carved out a legacy to be proud of inside and outside of the ring. I do hope you will enjoy this book.

This publication also looks at what happened to the careers of the boxers after they had fought Cooper in a title contest. The facts are presented in such a way that you will be able to dip in at any page and absorb information about Cooper's boxing career. Henry Cooper was a man who really was a great ambassador for the sport. Indeed, he was 'Our 'Enry'.

Ralph Oates

Chapter One
The Early Years

The Story Begins

The Henry Cooper story began on 3rd May 1934, when proud parents Lily and Henry Cooper Snr welcomed two new additions to their family in the shape of identical twin sons, whom they named Henry and George. Henry was the older of the two by a reported twenty minutes. The Coopers now had three sons in the household, the older sibling being Bern.

Champions at the Time of the Cooper Twins' Birth

At the time of Henry Cooper and George's birth, the reigning world heavyweight king was Italy's Primo Carnera, and the British and Commonwealth champion at the weight was Len Harvey. The Cooper family lived in a council House at Farmstead Road, Bellingham Estate in South-East London. However, their life was interrupted by the onset of World War II, and like so many at that time, they suffered the hardships that period presented.

A Plaque

In later years, a blue plaque was placed on the wall at the front of the house in Farmstead Road, which states that Henry Cooper had once lived there. The plaque also honoured the boxing achievements of Cooper.

Spotting the Potential

It was a fireman, Bob Hill, who noticed that Henry Cooper had the makings of being a good boxer. He observed the young Cooper sparring on a grass verge with friends. Hill had boxed for the fire brigade, so he had a degree of knowledge about the sport and knew potential when he saw it. He suggested that Cooper would benefit from joining the local boxing Club. Cooper duly joined the Bellingham Boxing Club, and later the Eltham Boxing Club.

Matt Wells

Matt Wells was one of the trainers who passed on his boxing knowledge to Henry Cooper at the Bellingham Boxing Club. Wells really knew his stuff, since during his professional career he had won the British title and had been involved in a number of high-profile bouts. That fact made him more than qualified to guide aspiring boxers.

ABA Light-Heavyweight Champion

Henry Cooper made an impression in the amateur ranks with his combination of both aggression and punching power. These were attributes which made him one to watch out for in the future. During his time in the unpaid code, Cooper won two ABA light-heavyweight titles. That is an outstanding achievement for any boxer.

He first won the title on 25th April 1952, out-pointing Scotland's John McLean over three rounds in the final of the championships, which was staged at the Empire Pool, Wembley, London.

Youngest Boxer

At just seventeen years, eleven months and twenty-two days old, Henry Cooper became the youngest boxer to win the ABA light-heavyweight championship when he defeated John McLean.

Tony Madigan

To win the ABA light-heavyweight crown for the second time, Cooper outpointed Tony Madigan of Australia over three rounds in the final of the championships in a bout which took place on 24th April 1953. The contest was also staged at the Empire Pool, Wembley, London.

In the Army

In their teenage years, the Cooper twins, like so many others, were conscripted into the army. They served with the Royal Army Ordnance Corps, and duly completed their two years of National Service.

However, while serving, they continued boxing, whereupon they impressed everyone with their skills. It was clear that they would have a career in the professional ring once their time in the army was over.

It's a Small World

We have all heard the expression, 'It's a small world'. Henry Cooper found this to be very true when serving in the army.

He was a little shocked when he found that his company sergeant-major was Mick Kavanagh, a man whom he had once stopped in two rounds in an amateur contest. This could have been very awkward for Cooper, but it wasn't. Kavanagh held no hard feelings towards his former conqueror.

The Olympic Games

Henry Cooper took part in the Olympic Games at light-heavyweight in 1952, the location for the competition being Helsinki, Finland. Cooper had what could be called a good start when he was given a 'bye' (advanced to the next round without having to fight) in the first round of the games. Despite this easy start, Cooper wasn't fated to go far in the event and hence failed to claim a medal. Cooper was duly eliminated in the next round of the competition when outpointed over three rounds. The opponent who defeated Cooper was Anatoly Perov of the Soviet Union, who went on to win a bronze medal. Norvel Lee of the USA won the gold medal in the division.

Gold Medal at Middleweight

At the same Olympics in which Henry competed, a boxer from the USA won the gold medal at middleweight when he knocked out Vasile Tita of Romania in the first round of three.

That boxer was Floyd Patterson, who would go on to become the first fighter in the history of the sport to win the world heavyweight title on two separate occasions. Another future world heavyweight king who fought at the same event was Ingemar Johansson from Sweden, who lost in the final against Ed Sanders of the USA, by way of a disqualification in round two. Patterson, Johansson, and Cooper would all eventually meet each other in the professional ranks.

Jim Wicks

Any boxer needs to have a good manager, and in Jim Wicks, Henry and Jim Cooper really struck gold. Wicks was a man who knew the fight game and was a respected figure in the sport. Wicks already had a successful stable of fighters in his charge prior to him taking on the Cooper twins.

The Bishop

Jim Wicks, nicknamed the 'Bishop', formed a strong bond with the Cooper twins and guided them throughout their careers. He always ensured, when negotiating with promoters, that his charges were treated fairly and given a fair shake.

Danny Holland

Trainer and cornerman Danny Holland was a vital cog in the early career of Henry Cooper. He was a man who ensured that both brothers were expertly put through their paces in the gym, not taking any shortcuts in their preparation. Holland was experienced in the role he played and became a legend in his own right in the boxing community. Holland was superb when dealing with any cuts which a fighter may have sustained during a bout. It was, without doubt, a big plus for a fighter to have Holland in their corner during a contest.

The Thomas A Becket

Henry and George were always in superb condition when they entered the ring to fight. Danny Holland prepared the fighters in a gym above a pub called the Thomas A Becket, which was situated on the Old Kent Road, London. The gym had seen a number of outstanding fighters frequent the premises over the years.

Plasterers

Both Henry and George wisely became Plasterers. It was necessary for them to take on a trade for obvious reasons. Boxing is a risky and unpredictable business at the best of times, and if the sport did not pay off for the twins, it was necessary for them to have a trade to fall back on later in life. Hence the old saying, 'don't put all your eggs in one basket'.

Chapter Two

A Step into the Professional Ranks

The Professional Debut

Henry Cooper entered the roped arena on 14th September 1954 at the Harringay Arena, Harringay, London, to have his first paid contest. The first outing in the professional ranks is always a little nerve-wracking for any boxer. There is always that lingering question in a fighter's mind – 'What if it all goes wrong, and I lose?'

Cooper's opponent coming out of the opposite corner was Hampshire's Harry Painter, whose record was twenty-seven bouts, winning twelve, losing fifteen. He was not a bad opponent for a fighter making his professional debut. Painter had lost his last three bouts on the bounce. In his last outing before his meeting with Cooper, he had been stopped in the second stanza of eight by Jack Darlington on 26th April 1954 at the Granby Halls Leicester, Leicestershire.

So it was odds on that Cooper would win this contest, but it was felt that Painter would give him some competitive rounds and extend him a little before eventually losing. Perhaps he might even be experienced enough to last the full course of the contest.

That view was wrong: the scheduled six-rounder ended in the opening session, when Cooper landed his left hook, knocking Painter out. There was no reconnaissance work carried out by Cooper, no looking to see what his opponent had to offer. He just went in and finished the job. This was an encouraging start by Cooper, who made a good impression on the punters in attendance. This proved to be Painter's last contest.

Cooper's Brother

On the Henry Cooper-Harry Painter card, Cooper's twin brother George also made his debut. He had now changed his name to Jim. The name change was made due to the fact that there was another heavyweight boxer at the time with the same name. Jim also had a successful introduction to the professional ranks when he defeated Welshman Dick Richardson, who was also making his professional debut.

However, he had to work a little harder than his sibling to acquire victory, having to go the full distance of six rounds to gain a points decision. It had been a good night for the Cooper twins, who could look back on the evening with a feeling of contentment, with the added relief of getting their first fights out of the way.

Jack Solomons

Jack Solomons was a major British boxing promoter who, during his long and successful career, brought a number of top names from the USA and other parts of the world to fight in Britain. He was, without doubt, the main man in the promoting field in the UK at that time. He had gained international prominence over the years by putting together major bouts. Solomons can also lay claim to being the first man to have promoted a Henry Cooper contest, hence the Harry Painter bout.

Second Professional Contest

It was back to Harringay Arena, Harringay, London on 19th October 1954 for Henry. The man gloved up in the opposite corner, and ready for action was Dinny Powell, whose record read twenty bouts consisting of six victories, eleven defeats, with three drawn. This was not an impressive slate, but no one would expect Cooper to be put in too deep at this early stage against a tough opponent. He was still new to the paid game and still had a great deal to learn.

A war with a more experienced fighter, one who would take him into the trenches, was not on the agenda. Powell was the sensible choice to further the Londoners' ring education. In his last contest, which had taken place on 26th April 1954, Powell had outpointed Bob Gardner over six rounds at the Granby Halls, Leicester, Leicestershire.

So the man facing Cooper was coming in with a win behind him. The win would have more than bolstered Powell's confidence in his outing against Cooper. He no doubt held the belief that he just might spring a surprise on the night and add another victory to his name. Cooper was only human, and there was nothing to suggest at this stage that he could not be beaten. He was, in professional terms, still a novice.

However, truth be told, the fight with Powell did not look like it was going to be too taxing for Cooper, and so it proved.

The contest lasted longer than his first bout, but it still ended early. Powell was made to order for Cooper, who kept his undefeated resumé intact. He was punch-perfect against his opponent, and soon found his range to claim victory in the fourth stanza of a scheduled six.

Another One Round Victory

It was soon time for Henry Cooper to slip between the ropes and box once again.

On 23rd November 1954, Eddie Keith was the opponent who stepped into the square ring to meet the undefeated boxer. Keith came to the Manor Place Baths, Walworth, London, with a resumé of three bouts, winning two and losing one.

Like Cooper, Keith was new to the professional ranks and was keen to impress. In his last bout, which had taken place on 1st June 1954, he fought a man who was destined to play a large part in Cooper's fistic career: Welshman Joe Erskine. Keith and Erskine had met in a semi-final novice competition, which had been staged at White City Stadium, London. Keith was halted by Erskine in the second stanza of a scheduled three-round contest.

Erskine went on to win the tournament, out-pointing Denny Ball over three rounds, and he showed his ring skills in doing so. Erskine was sending out a message to the boxing world that he was one to watch, a real prospect, a man destined for big things.

Keith was keen to get his career back on track after the Erskine setback, and a win over Cooper would do the trick. Cooper was not feeling in a benevolent mood on the night and did the job quicker than Erskine, ending the bout by stopping Keith in the opening stanza in a bout set for six. Cooper hardly raised a sweat in gaining what was a very easy victory. This gave him a slight psychological edge over his rival Erskine.

Cooper Continues Run of Quick Wins

Henry Cooper's next foray into the ring took place on 7th December 1954, against Denny Ball, who entered the fray with a resumé of eight bouts, with five victories and three defeats. This was not a bad record, one which suggested that Ball might make things a little interesting for Cooper, giving him a problem or two during their encounter.

Last time out, Ball had fought South African Colin Strauch on 22nd November 1954 at the Hippodrome, Great Yarmouth, Norfolk, where he boxed his way to a six round points victory over his opponent.

The Cooper-Ball contest took place at the Harringay Arena, Harringay, London. Cooper did not want to hang around for too long in the ring that night, and so, he introduced his opponent to a very good friend of his: the left hook, which, when landed, showed Ball the exit door – he was knocked out in round three of six, ending the year on a high note. It was a case of onwards and upwards for Cooper.

Royal Albert Hall Debut

Henry next fought at the Royal Albert Hall, Kensington, London on 27th January 1955, his opponent being South African-born Colin Strauch. This looked like an interesting contest, since Strauch was the most experienced fighter Cooper had met at this stage of his career. The South

African held a resumé which consisted of thirty-six bouts, winning fifteen, losing nineteen, with two defeats. Before sharing the ring with Cooper, Strauch had last fought on 4th December 1954 at the Ulster Hall, Belfast, Northern Ireland, against Garnett Denny.

In this bout, Strauch suffered a defeat when stopped in round seven of eight. Despite the fact that Strauch had made a number of visits to the ring, no one felt that he was going to defeat Cooper – maybe push him a little for a couple of rounds or so, before going down to defeat.

Cooper, in fact, did not need to go a couple of rounds to beat his opponent. He brought the curtain down on the planned six-round bout, stopping his opponent in the opening stanza, sending him for an early shower. It could be said that this was a very generous act by Cooper, since this quick victory ensured that his fans would not miss the last train or bus home.

It was the kind of fight where if you blinked or looked away for a moment, you missed it. This was a good start to the year by Cooper, but not so good for Strauch.

Chapter Three
First Professional Defeat

Going the Distance for The First Time

It was back to the Harringay Arena, Harringay, London, for Henry on 8th February 1955, where he was set to face opponent Cliff Purnell. In his previous bout on 24th January 1955, Purnell had knocked out Terry McDonald in round four of eight at the Kings Hall, Derby, Derbyshire.

So he was coming to battle Cooper with a handy win behind him, one which would give him confidence in this contest.

During his time in the sport, Purnell had put together a record of twenty-five bouts, which consisted of fourteen victories, ten defeats, and one draw. When looking at the contest between the two boxers, it looked as if Cooper would secure another inside-the-distance win once his left hook came into play. Should Purnell feel the full force of the punch, it would consequently separate him from his senses and put him to sleep.

However, Purnell surprised the pundits when he made Cooper work harder than he had in his previous outings. He was no sitting duck – he knew his way around the ring and became the first man in the professional ranks to take Cooper the distance in the six-round scheduled bout. A stoppage win by Cooper would have been welcomed by his fans, who were used to seeing him put his opponents away.

Ultimately, it was good for him to get some rounds under his belt and, in so doing, get the experience of going the full distance in a contest. He would now appreciate that not all opponents will fold in the heat of battle.

Disappointing Contest

The next bout for Henry Cooper came on 8th March 1955, in a contest which took place at Earl's Court Arena, Kensington, London. The opponent gloved up in the opposing corner was Hugh Ferns from Scotland. Cooper was more than keen to continue with his winning ways and punch his way to an impressive victory.

The anticipation of an exciting bout between Cooper and Ferns was soon quelled. The fight was somewhat disappointing, since it failed to catch fire; in fact, it didn't even smoulder. Ferns took to the ring with a record of nineteen fights, with twelve victories and seven defeats. In his last foray into the ring, Ferns had stepped in with Peter Bates on 4th October 1954, the venue for said bout being Farrer Street Stadium, Middlesborough, Yorkshire. It was not a successful venture for Ferns, since he was stopped in the fourth round of eight.

When considering the outcome of this contest, it looked as if Ferns would end up defeated well before the final bell had tolled. Ferns had indeed reached this stage, but not in the way it was expected. The fight was scheduled for six rounds, but it came to a close when Ferns was disqualified in the second stanza for misuse of the head. This was not the way Cooper would have wanted to win, but realistically, a win is a win, and at the end of the day, that is what counts.

Quick Return to the Ring

Cooper returned quickly to the ring after the win over Hugh Ferns, which really was a non-event. The opponent this time facing Cooper was Joe Crickmar, who came with a slate of sixteen bouts, consisting of eight victories and eight defeats.

In his last bout, which had taken place on 28th February 1955, Crickmar lost an eight-round points decision to Joe Erskine at the Granby Halls, Leicester. Erskine, like Cooper, was an up-and-coming heavyweight hope who was also making good progress in the domestic heavyweight division.

It seemed like it was only a matter of time before Erskine and Cooper would go nose to nose in the ring. A meeting between the two would be an exciting prospect, certainly one which would entice the fans to part with their hard-earned money and purchase a ticket. The bout between Cooper and Crickmar was scheduled for eight rounds. This was the first time Cooper had fought in a contest set for this distance, and he was more than ready to rumble and notch up another win.

The encounter between the pair took place at Earl's Court Arena, Kensington, London, on 29th March 1955. Cooper was on his game: he showed his skills and punching power in no uncertain way, to claim another victory, when he methodically stopped Crickmar in the fifth session. To some extent, this must have given Cooper a certain amount of satisfaction – being able to once again stop a fighter who had taken Erskine the full distance in a contest.

First Time Going Eight Rounds

On 18th April 1955, Henry Cooper entered the ring at Manor Place Baths, Walworth, London, to battle Jamaican-born Joe Bygraves, who had a record consisting of twenty-nine bouts, consisting of twenty-four wins and five defeats. This wasn't a bad resumé, and it really looked as if Bygraves would give Cooper a hard fight. Bygraves had shown in past bouts that he was no pushover. He always came to fight and would slug it out to the very end.

Bygraves did not possess a loser's mentality when entering the ring. He was made of stern stuff – a quality he had revealed in previous outings during his career. Bygraves was a smart boxer. He had good defensive skills, backed up with solid punching power.

In his bout before meeting Cooper, he had lost an eight-round points decision to Polly Smith on 4th November 1954. The venue for the Bygraves-Smith contest was The Stadium, Liverpool, Merseyside.

This result had no bearing on his meeting with Cooper. If anything, the loss to Smith would make Bygraves even more determined to put his opponent's name in his win column. Bygraves was aware that Cooper was the favourite with the fans. He was the fighter on the way up, the one with the future. It was obvious that the spectators who came to watch their contest would be fully behind Cooper, cheering his every move. He was very much their man.

There were no two ways about it – Cooper was the star of the show, and Bygraves was very much the supporting act. This fact did not deter Bygraves in any way. If anything, it made him even more fired up to gain a victory. The Jamaican had every intention of upsetting the apple cart to show that he shouldn't be written off without any hope, and show that he too had a bright future in the sport.

In the contest with Cooper, Bygraves demonstrated his ring savvy, and in so doing, went the full distance of eight rounds, losing by a points decision. Cooper pressed the fight, but Bygraves used the ring well and was able to avoid the famed left hook, which Cooper had in his arsenal. This was the first time that Cooper had travelled the eight-round distance in a contest. He worked hard to obtain the victory, but the experience gained from the contest would serve him well in his future endeavours inside the ring.

Italian Shocks Cooper

It was going so well for Henry Cooper. He was moving up the rankings, looking to be the real deal. He was unaware when he got out of bed that morning on the 26th April 1955 that there was there was a disappointment waiting for him at the Harringay Arena, Harringay, London.

Cooper suffered his first defeat in the professional ranks. The man to inflict the loss was Italian Uber Bacilieri, who had put together a resumé of twenty-seven bouts, which consisted of fourteen wins, seven defeats and six draws.

In his bout before meeting Cooper, he had drawn with fellow countryman Giannino Orlando Luise over eight rounds on 14th April 1955. The venue for the Baciliert-Luise bout was the Badia Polesine, Veneto, Italy. The Italian was not exactly a fighter to be fearful of, but he was a competent enough opponent. It was felt that the visitor would give a good account of himself against Cooper before eventually being taken out before the final bell had sounded. A case of 'another one bites the dust'.

There was little to indicate Bacilieri would leave the ring a victor on the night. To have predicted a win for the Italian fighter before the contest would have been a foolish call to make. In short, it was never going to happen. Not in a million years! Cooper was by far the superior fighter in all departments. It really looked like a routine outing for the British fighter. Yet, boxing has a way of making even the very best experts in the game look as if they know very little about the sport.

There was a nasty shock in store for the British fans who confidently expected Cooper to maintain his undefeated record and advance to the next level.

In the second stanza, the fight was stopped when Cooper sustained a cut over his eye, whereupon the blood ran down his face. Before the wound, it really looked as if Cooper was on his way to another win. His imperious left jab was finding its target every time it was thrown. The Italian was a spirited fighter, but he had little in his boxing skills to trouble the British fighter. Cooper moved well, picking his punches with precision. He looked a class above his opponent. Cooper was the boss inside the ring – it looked like it was only a matter of time before he extended his undefeated record.

However, the cut altered the course of the fight, changing what looked to be a certain victory into a defeat. It was not the end of the world for Cooper, but it was an unwanted setback, one which he could well have done without at the time. The wheels may have come off the bus, but Cooper left the ring determined to get back on to the victory trail.

Cooper Back in Action

After a suitable time away from the ring to let the cut heal, Henry Cooper returned to action on 6th June 1955. The venue for his return was the Ice Rink, Nottingham, Nottinghamshire.

His opponent was fellow Briton Ron Harman, who came with a record of sixteen fights, with fourteen wins, one defeat and one draw. That was a pretty good resumé, one which suggested that this contest might be a tough one for Cooper. Harman had sampled the atmosphere of a big-time fight in his last bout on 16th May 1955.

On that occasion, he fought at the Kezar Stadium, San Francisco, California, USA. He appeared on the undercard, which saw Rocky Marciano make a successful defence of his world heavyweight title, stopping Briton Don Cockell in round nine of fifteen. Harman had an easy night when he stopped his opponent, Bill Mathis in the first stanza of a four-round contest. Mathis was no great shakes – that was apparent from his slate, which read fifteen bouts, consisting of three wins, eleven defeats and one draw, but still, a win away from home in the states looked good on the record.

Harman was confident that he had the beating of Cooper and would add another victory to his record. He was not entering the ring to be cannon fodder for Cooper; he had his own ambitions in the sport – he wanted to advance his career, and winning this fight would certainly help him climb the domestic ratings. While showing some good moves during the bout, Harman was unable to find his rhythm, and he determined that Cooper was a much tougher fighter than Bill Mathis. He was ultimately broken down and removed from the equation when Cooper halted him in round seven of eight. All in all, it was a good display by Cooper.

Time for Revenge

Henry Cooper ducked between the ropes at the White City Stadium, White City, London, on 13th September 1955. It was time to right a wrong and set the record straight with Italian opponent Uber Bacilieri, who had stopped him on 26th April 1955, in the second round of eight, by way of a cut-eye decision.

In defeating Cooper, Bacilieri had pulled off what was considered to be a shock victory over the British fighter. Their bout had taken place at Harringay Arena, Harringay, London. In his previous bout before meeting Cooper in this return contest, Bacilieri had lost a ten-round points decision to Welshman Joe Erskine – the man who was keeping pace with Cooper's progress.

The venue for the Erskine-Bacilieri bout was the Maindy Stadium, Cardiff, Wales. The bout had taken place on 29th August 1955. Since his contest with Cooper, Bacilieri had fought five times, winning three and losing two. This brought his resumé of contests to thirty-three bouts, winning eighteen, losing nine, with six drawn.

For the first time, Cooper fought in a contest set for the duration of ten rounds. He didn't need to travel that distance. It's often said that revenge is sweet; if that's true, then Cooper must have had a large jar of honey on the night to savour. He enthusiastically went about his task, using his educated left jab to keep his man on the back foot.

Cooper was cheered on by the fans and finally brought the show to a finish when he knocked his opponent out in round seven. He left the ring that night feeling happy with his work, while the Italian went home with another loss on his record.

Chapter Four
Cooper's Bad Run

The Eliminator

The British Heavyweight Championship was now within touching distance for Henry Cooper. In his next contest, he was matched in a final eliminator for the title. So Cooper had just one final hurdle to clear before he was able to challenge for the British crown.

That hurdle, of course, being Welshman Joe Erskine – a fighter whom he was now to exchange punches with inside the ring. It would not be easy to overcome the hurdle, as Erskine was one smart cookie. It had been obvious for some time that Cooper and Erskine would eventually meet in the professional ranks.

The showdown *had* to happen: the fight was a natural between two domestic heavyweight hopes. The event would pull in the punters, much to the delight of the promoter staging the fight. Erskine had the kind of skills which were much admired by a number of boxing connoisseurs. The Welshman could box like a dream when the night was his, showing why the sport is often called the 'sweet science'.

He had a stiff left jab, but it lacked the power that Cooper possessed, which was deemed in some quarters as a disadvantage.

The match between Cooper and Erskine looked to be intriguing: it was a fifty-fifty affair, one where it was difficult to pick a clear-cut winner. You certainly wouldn't want to bet your last dollar, or your house, on predicting who the victor would be on the night, after the last punch had been thrown.

In the bout before meeting Cooper, Erskine had swapped punches with Al Bernard of Belgium on 10th October 1955, at Sophia Gardens Pavilion, Cardiff, Wales. The fight was set for ten rounds, but was halted in the second stanza in favour of Erskine.

During his time punching for pay, Erskine had garnered a total of twenty-five bouts, winning twenty-four with one drawn. By comparison, Cooper had fought on twelve occasions, winning eleven and losing one.

The fight with Cooper would be Erskine's eleventh of the year. He was a very active fighter, to say the least. When looking at their resumés, it was clear that Erskine had the edge in experience over Cooper. On 15th November 1955, Cooper and Erskine entered the ring and confronted each other at the Harringay Arena, Harringay, London. Erskine, as expected, boxed well from the opening round and looked every inch a class act.

As the rounds rolled by, the Welshman maintained control of the contest. Cooper looked to be heading for his second professional defeat – a fact which became evident during the early stages of the contest. Erskine was quick and anticipated Cooper's every move during the bout, and he was able to constantly pierce his defence. The Welshman clearly had a good boxing IQ and looked special, every inch a future British champion. Erskine looked capable of going even further than the domestic title in the fullness of time. The talent was there to be seen. There could be no argument about who the winner was when the fight came to a close.

The Welshman's hand was raised in victory after earning a ten-round points decision. Erskine was clearly delighted with the win. He had seen-off his rival in style and would now go forward for a title shot.

The defeat was an obvious disappointment for Cooper, but he couldn't dwell on the loss. On the night, Erskine was the better man. Cooper showed dignity in defeat and revealed he had the potential to come back again. Cooper had been outsmarted and out-boxed by Erskine, but he would learn from the loss, get over it and come back a better fighter at a later date. Boxers win and boxers lose. That is the nature of the sport.

Mols No Match for Cooper

At the Royal Albert Hall, Kensington, London, Henry returned to the ring to meet French heavyweight title holder Maurice Mols on 28th February 1956. Mols came with a record of twenty-three bouts, winning ten, losing ten, with three drawn.

The visitor didn't look to be too much of a threat to Cooper. In his previous venture between the ropes, Mols had outpointed Robert Eugene of Belgium over ten rounds at the Palais de la Mutualite, Paris, France, in a contest which took place on 22nd January, 1956. Cooper was smarting over his defeat to Erskine, which had taken place in his previous bout and was keen to get back to his winning ways. The Frenchman looked the ideal opponent for Cooper, who looked a good bet to punch his way to victory.

Cooper not only had to win, but win impressively – a dull performance would not go down well with the fans. When the two men left their corners, both looked a little pensive before they decided to let their hands go. Should Mols claim a victory over Cooper, he would return across the channel with a useful win under his belt, one which would bolster his reputation.

This gave the Frenchman a powerful incentive for boxing his way to a victory. Cooper, too, had more than his share of incentive to obtain a win in this bout. He couldn't afford to slip up and lose. The last thing he wanted was another loss on his record.

On the night, Cooper was in no mood to let that happen, or indeed let the Frenchman hang around for too long in this contest. The quicker he got rid of his opponent, the better. Mols had no idea what was in store for him or how quickly his night would come to an end. If he did, the Frenchman might very well have decided to stay in France under the shadow of the Eiffel Tower.

From the off, Cooper was workmanlike in his approach to Mols, promptly erasing the memory of his last loss to Joe Erskine. He hunted down his man like a lion stalking his prey, and won in no uncertain manner. Cooper stopped the Frenchman in round four of ten.

Overall, it was a pleasing performance by the British fighter, one which showed (despite his defeat to Erskine) that he still had a great deal to offer the sport. Cooper was still on the championship trail. It was a case of to write Cooper off was to do so at your own peril.

London Beaten by Cooper

Henry Cooper's next task was to meet Brian London, who was undefeated in twelve bouts, winning eleven inside the distance, confirming that he had some power in his punches – a fact which had to be taken into consideration when predicting who would come out of the clash with a victory.

Looking at the contest, this didn't look like an easy outing for Cooper. In fact, it looked like a risky one for him. A defeat was a possibility against London: you could not write the man from Blackpool off. He was one dangerous fighter.

London, too, had his eyes on the domestic title, and by crushing Cooper, he would be sending out the message that he was ready to step up and contest the title. In his previous bout before facing Cooper, London had stopped fighter José Peyre of Belgium in the opening round of ten, on 13th March 1956. Peyre was nowhere near world-class, but nevertheless, the way London dismissed him was impressive.

The London-Peyre contest had taken place at the Harringay Arena, Harringay, London. An interesting footnote, which helped to create even more interest in the Cooper-London encounter, was on 17th January 1956, London had stopped Jim Cooper (Henry's brother) in round four of ten. That fight's location was the Streatham Ice Rink, Streatham, London.

The contest between London and Cooper took place at the Earls Court Empress Hall, Kensington, London, on 1st May 1966.

It could be said that Cooper had a score to settle with London. Settle it he did, in devastating fashion when he caught London with his sleep-inducing left hook in the first stanza of ten.

London didn't see it coming; the punch was fast and accurate. London did not fall to the canvas – he remained on his feet, but he was out. His eyes were vacant. It could be said that the lights were on, but there was no one at home.

For a brief moment, London had been introduced to astronomy, for he most certainly saw stars from the impact of the blow from Cooper. London's undefeated resumé had come to an abrupt and brutal end. The referee correctly intervened and stopped the bout.

One didn't need to be a boxing expert to know that London could not go on – he was finished for the evening, and it was thus time to say goodnight and go home. The Cooper family pride had been well and truly restored.

Italian Feels the Power of Cooper

Italian Giannino Orlando Luise climbed the steps into the ring at the Empire Pool, Wembley, London, on 26th June 1956, to meet Henry Cooper in a ten-round contest. Luise was no mug; he had a good-looking resumé of twenty-three bouts, winning nineteen and losing three, with one drawn.

Prior to meeting Cooper, Luise had stopped Horst Herold of Germany in round six of eight at Padu, Veneto, Italy on 31st May 1956. The Italian had every intention of adding another victory to his name and going back home to sunny Italy a winner.

Cooper had a determined look on his face when he left his corner and soon had the measure of his opponent. His classy left hand landed frequently on the visitor, who was often rocked back on his feet by the force of the jabs. Luise was out of his league against Cooper, and deep down inside, he must have known it. There was little he could do to turn the tide and get the better of the British fighter.

Cooper was on his A game. He was on fire. He fought well, giving a hard-hitting performance against his opponent. The Italian showed bravery, but that attribute wasn't enough. Not against a fighter like Cooper. Bravery can only get you so far inside the ring.

Cooper put another win in his column when he defeated the Italian in round seven of ten, when the referee stopped the bout. Luise, after being floored, got to his feet, but he was clearly discombobulated and in no fit state to continue the battle.

At that moment, he probably didn't know what his name was, what day it was, or even what month it was, such was the impact of the blow he took from Cooper.

Luise must have thought after the fight, 'Mamma Mia! This man can really punch!' A number of Cooper's former opponents would not have disagreed with that sentiment.

Shock Defeat for Cooper

After his victory over Italian Giannino Orlando Luise, Henry looked ready to march on and add another win to his record. He travelled to Lancashire to meet Peter Bates on 7th September 1956.

It was a trip which ended in bitter disappointment for the Londoner. He suffered an unexpected defeat against Bates. The venue for the Cooper-Bates contest was the Kings Hall, Belle Vue, Manchester. Bates had previously taken part in twenty-nine bouts, winning twenty-two, losing six and drawing one. Bates was not a bad fighter – he was an accomplished boxer who always gave opponents a testing time.

However, Cooper was odds-on to win this bout and go home a happy man when their business was finished. It could not be overlooked that Bates had some history with the Cooper family.

On 28th February 1956, Bates had defeated Henry's brother Jim when he knocked him out in round two of eight at the Royal Albert Hall, Kensington, London. No doubt Cooper had this very much in mind on the night and would have more than enjoyed getting revenge for his brother. Many observers felt that it would only be a matter of time during the fight before Bates would feel the full power of Cooper's left hook, and that would be that – game over.

However, it didn't work out that way. Cooper was stopped in round five of ten, due to a badly cut eye. Before the injury, Cooper looked composed and on course to add another victory to his resumé. Bates now had the satisfaction of having scored a double over the Cooper twins.

Before his bout with Cooper, Bates had lost a ten-round points decision on 1st July 1956 to former European heavyweight champion Heinz Neuhaus in Germany, the venue for the contest being Wesfalenhalle, Dortmund, Nordrhein-Westfalen. In this outing, Bates had put in a more than credible performance against the tough German boxer before being defeated.

Bygraves Wins by a Knockout

On 19th February 1957, Henry Cooper had his first crack at a major title when he met Joe Bygraves for the

Commonwealth heavyweight title at Earl's Court Arena, Kensington, London. This looked to be a good opportunity for Cooper to shake off the defeat he suffered in his last contest to Peter Bates and to get back on the victory trail. Cooper was raring to go – he had previously defeated Bygraves in a bout which had taken place on 18th April 1955.

On that occasion, Cooper won by an eight-round points decision at the Manor Place Baths, Walworth, London. Since that defeat, Bygraves had been busy and had fought on thirteen occasions, winning ten and losing three.

Bygraves had won the vacant Commonwealth title on 26th June 1956, when he outpointed Tonga-born Kitione Lave over fifteen rounds at the Empire Pool, Wembley, London. That was a good win, which boosted Bygraves stock somewhat in the world of boxing.

In his bout before meeting Cooper, Bygraves had, on 16th November 1956, defeated former British and Commonwealth heavyweight king Johnny Williams, who retired in round six of ten at Kings Hall, Belle Vue, Manchester, Lancashire. On record, this looked to be an impressive name to have beaten. Williams was good in his day; there was no doubt about that, but now he was past his best, and this bout had proven to be his last. He later hung up his gloves and said goodbye to the sport. So not too much could be taken from that win by the Jamaican-born fighter.

The fight against Cooper was the first defence of the Commonwealth title by Bygraves. The champion was confident that he would reverse his previous defeat to Cooper and retain the crown.

On the night, there was a good-sized crowd rooting for

Cooper. They felt that he would box the ears off Bygraves and take the title, if not indeed stop him inside the distance. The challenger eyed the champion from his corner, taking stock of the man he was now set to battle with. He fully realised that winning this championship was important to his career.

When the bell sounded to start the contest, Bygraves sprang out of his corner and looked menacing, marching forward, looking to unload on his challenger.

The champion had early success scoring with stiff punches to both the head and body of Cooper. Bygraves had made a good start, stamping his authority on the contest. Cooper seemed to have difficulty finding his range against Bygraves with his left jab; he couldn't quite get his timing right. Bygraves was moving his head and slipping his challenger's jabs with considerable ease.

There was no doubt that Cooper was struggling against the defending title holder. He just couldn't pin him down. The generalisation that Cooper would repeat his win over Bygraves was proving to be incorrect. The fight was gradually slipping away from Cooper, bit by bit. There was the faint hope that the challenger might turn the fight around, once his left hook struck home. That would be a game-changer, but the punch didn't materialise.

It wasn't Cooper's night. Little, if anything, was going right for him. Bygraves was a much-improved fighter from the man Cooper had previously fought. He was very focused and on top of his game, not taking his eyes off his challenger for one minute. In round nine, the fight came to a dramatic finish when a battle-weary Cooper was knocked out in the scheduled fifteen-round bout. Bygraves had landed a heavy punch to the stomach of Cooper, taking all the fight out of him, and sending him to the canvas to be counted out by the referee.

When looking at the way the fight was panning out, the defeat of Cooper came as no surprise when it eventually came. Bygraves had retained his crown, and he did so in some style. He was delighted with the win – a win which served as a warning to fellow heavyweights that he was one serious fighter, and not one to be taken lightly.

The loss was a shattering blow for Cooper, who was obviously disappointed at the outcome. The title would have been a boost for his career. Holding the championship would have elevated his position in the rankings to some degree. The crown would have also been a good bargaining tool when negotiating future fights. The big question now was: 'What next for Cooper?'

Bygraves' Last Contest

After making a successful Commonwealth title defence against Henry Cooper, Joe Bygraves took to the ring another twenty-eight times, winning seven, losing nineteen and drawing two.

He entered the fray for the last time on 20th March 1967, the venue for the bout being the Hilton Hotel (Anglo American Sporting Club), Mayfair, London. His opponent was Eduardo Corletti of Argentina. Bygraves lost the contest to Corletti when he was outpointed over the duration of ten rounds. Bygraves was a well-respected fighter. His retirement saw a colourful boxing career come to an end.

During his career, Bygraves participated in seventy-two bouts, of which he won forty-two, with twenty-eight defeats and two draws.

Solomons the First

The Joe Bygraves vs. Henry Cooper Commonwealth heavyweight title bout was promoted by Jack Solomons. On this occasion, Solomons became the first man to promote Cooper in a championship bout.

Ingemar Johansson

The defeat in his Commonwealth heavyweight title challenge against Joe Bygraves was a bitter disappointment for Henry Cooper. It was a fight he felt he should have won.

However, a ray of sunshine shone through the darkness for Cooper. He was presented with another title opportunity. He was to challenge for the European Heavyweight Championship. The reigning title holder at the time was Ingemar Johansson. It wouldn't be easy for Cooper to take the crown, that was for sure.

When looking at the contest without the use of rose-tinted glasses, it looked as if Cooper was heading for another defeat against the heavily favoured Swedish boxer. Johansson was a budding star in Sweden. He was a fighter who looked on course for bigger and better things in the boxing world. It was generally felt that Johansson would brush Cooper aside without any undue difficulty, then search for more lucrative fights.

Rightly or wrongly, Cooper was not considered to be any kind of threat to the champion. Neither Johansson nor his management team would suffer from loss of sleep at the prospect of going into the ring with the British fighter.

Admittedly, Cooper always had a puncher's chance against Johansson, but would that be enough for him to topple the champion?

Having to travel to Sweden to challenge Johansson on his own ground was going to make his task even more problematic. This was the first time that Cooper had left UK shores to fight abroad while boxing in the professional ranks. Johansson was undefeated in sixteen outings and was known to be a big puncher, having won ten (including one on a disqualification) of his fights inside the distance.

Johansson had taken the title in impressive style on 30th September 1956, when he knocked out the then title holder, Italian Franco Cavicchi, in round thirteen of fifteen. The battleground for the Johansson-Cavicchi fight had been the Stadio Comunale, Bologna, Emilia, Romagna, Italy. The victory over Cavicchi highlighted Johansson's potential and slotted him into the category of a fighter who was a little special.

On the night, Johansson became Sweden's first holder of the championship since Olle Tandberg. Tandberg won the title when he outpointed Belgium's Karel Sys over fifteen rounds, for the vacant crown in a bout which had taken place on 30th May 1943. The venue for the Tandberg-Sys contest was the Rasunda, Solna, Sweden. Tandberg did not have time to settle into the role of being a champion, since he lost the title in his first defence on 14th November 1943. The loss of the championship came when he met Sys in a return bout at the Palais des Sports, Schaerbeek. Bruxelles-Capitale in Belgium. The defeat came by way of a fifteen-round points decision.

By bringing the European championship back to Sweden, Johansson became a hero to his countrymen.

Before his bout with Cooper, Johansson had looked in fine form on 28th December 1956, knocking out another

Brit, Peter Bates, in round two of a scheduled ten at Masshallen, Gotenburg, Sweden. Bates had defeated Cooper on 7th September 1956, at Kings Hall, Belle Vue, Manchester, stopping him in round five of ten by way of a cut eye.

Cooper stepped into the open-air ring on 19th May 1957 at Johanneshov Ice Stadium, Stockholm, to face Johansson, and showed little concern about the job that lay ahead of him. He was given a cool reception by the fans, which was expected. Cooper had a mountain to climb, and it was a steep mountain, make no mistake. Cooper was under no illusions about the difficult task he had in front of him.

When the bell sounded to start the action, the two fighters took a long look at each other, not being too quick to commit. As the rounds ticked by, Cooper got into his stride and looked good, scoring with a good jarring left jab which found its target.

For a time, the jab put the champion on the back foot – he had a healthy respect for the power Cooper had in his famed left hook. It seemed that Cooper might, after all, be in with a slight chance of taking the title back to the UK.

Upsets do happen in the fight game, and this might be a contest which would provide one of those upsets. It would be a magical occasion for both Cooper and British boxing if that were to be the case. A win would really put Cooper back in the mainstream of boxing.

The fight game, however, can be a real heartbreaker. It can lift you and tear you down in an instant. One cannot count their chickens too soon, or get too far ahead of themselves, when inside the ring. The determined champion had no intention of finishing in second place.

The contest came to a close when Johansson ensured the title remained in Swedish hands by knocking out Cooper in round five, courtesy of his right hand, which blasted its way to its target. There was no coming back from that punch – it would have knocked out any man in the heavyweight division.

The end had come dramatically and was most welcomed by the home fans. They were pleased with their man's performance, which confirmed that he was the best fighter in Europe, and one of the best in the world. It was good for Sweden to have a fighter like Johansson in their midst – he was giving the sport a massive boost in the country. It was known before the fight that both fighters had the power in their mitts to finish the show early if the opportunity presented itself. So no one was surprised by the early finish. It would have been more of a surprise had the bout gone the distance.

At that moment, Cooper was not in a good place career-wise. There was a great deal for him to mull over in the months to come.

Swedish Promoter

Swedish-born Edwin Ahiqvist was the promoter of the Ingemar Johansson-Henry Cooper European heavyweight title contest. Hence Ahiqvist can lay claim to being the first man to promote a European championship fight which involved Cooper.

'Enry's 'Ammer and Ingo's Bingo

Henry Cooper's left hook was known as ''Enry's 'Ammer' – a dangerous punch which could end a contest if it found its target. Ingemar Johansson had a dangerous right hand, which could also bring an end to a contest once it landed. The said right hand of the Swedish fighter had three nicknames, these being 'Ingo's Bingo', 'The Hammer of Thor' and 'Toonder and Lightning'. Whatever nickname anyone applied to Johansson's punch, all who were on the receiving end would agree it was one hell of a blow.

Long Wait for Medal

Ingemar Johansson had competed at the heavyweight level in the Olympic Games, which had taken place in Helsinki, Finland, in 1952. He fought his way to the final, but failed to secure a medal when he was disqualified in round two against Ed Sanders of the USA for not giving his best. Just when he thought things couldn't get any worse, a further disappointment was bestowed on him when he found his silver medal had been withheld.

So he returned to Sweden with nothing but a bad memory – one which would remain with him for a number of years. However, he was eventually presented with the medal some years later in 1982.

Became World Heavyweight Champion

Losing to Ingemar Johansson was not exactly a high moment in the life of Henry Cooper. He could take some comfort in the knowledge that he had been defeated by a man who would later shock the world. If not shock the world, then send tremors of disbelief through the sport.

In his fifth contest after beating Cooper, Johansson travelled to the USA to challenge Floyd Patterson for the world heavyweight crown. Critics felt it was a lost cause and thought he would return home to Sweden empty-handed, a well-beaten fighter, another European who had stepped out of his class and paid the ultimate price for doing so.

On 26th June 1959, Johansson showed he was one serious fighter when he stopped Patterson in the third round of fifteen to take the championship. The spectators who came to witness the fight felt it would be over very quickly – no way was this bout going the distance. No way was this challenger going to take the title home.

The bout would be very short and very sweet, with the American world champion being victorious. They were right with the first assessment; it was very short and very sweet, but they were wrong about who the victor would be when the fight was over. The sporting scribes could not believe what they had just witnessed at the Yankee Stadium, The Bronx, New York. The title had left the USA; this was not supposed to happen. This was not in the script. Everyone knew that the world heavyweight title belonged in the USA; that it was American property.

A return bout between Patterson and Johansson eventually took place on 20th June 1960, at the Polo Grounds, New York. Patterson vowed to bring the title back into American hands, and he was as good as his word. In an explosive encounter, he knocked Johansson out in the fifth stanza of fifteen.

In doing so, he became the first man to regain the world heavyweight crown – a truly historical occasion for the sport. A third fight between the two had to happen. The two fighters stepped into the Convention Center, Miami Beach, Florida, USA on 13th March 1961. The bout proved to be a hard-hitting and exciting contest, one which saw Patterson retain the title when he knocked out Johansson in the sixth stanza.

The bout was scheduled for fifteen rounds, but in a fight where both men were noted punchers, and based on their first two bouts, no way this contest was going the distance.

Primo Carnera

In defeating Floyd Patterson, Ingemar Johansson became the first European boxer to win the world heavyweight title since Italy's Primo Carnera, who won the championship on 29th June 1933, by defeating the holder Jack Sharkey by way of a six-round knockout in a scheduled fifteen.

The contest took place at the Madison Square Garden Bowl, Long Island City, Queens, New York. The championship returned to the States on 14th June 1934, when Max Baer stopped Carnera in round eleven in a bout set for a duration of fifteen. It was Carnera's third defence of the title.

The venue for the bout was once again Madison Square Garden Bowl.

Three World Title Fights in Succession

The Floyd Patterson-Ingemar Johansson bout, which took place on 13th March 1961, created a new page in the history books of boxing, since it was the first time that the same two fighters had fought on three successive occasions for the world championship in the heavyweight division.

Johansson's Last Professional Contest

After making a successful defence of his European heavyweight title against Henry Cooper, Ingemar Johansson took to the ring a further eleven times, winning nine and losing two. His last professional contest took place on 21st April 1963, against former British and Commonwealth heavyweight title holder Brian London.

The venue for Johansson-London bout was the Johanneshov Ice Stadium, Stockholm, Sweden. After twelve rounds of boxing, Johansson emerged the victor on points. While taking the decision, his performance was not one to inspire confidence in Johansson being able to maintain his position as a world-level fighter. It appeared that his best fighting years were behind him. Johansson's decision to walk away from the sport looked to be a wise move.

During his career, Ingemar Johansson took part in twenty-eight professional bouts, of which he won twenty-six and lost two.

Third Championship Chance

On 17th September 1957, Henry Cooper fought for his third championship when he took to the ring to challenge Joe Erskine for the British heavyweight title. This was a lifeline of a sort for Cooper; a victory here would salvage his now flagging fistic career. These were desperate times for Cooper. He needed a win, and he needed it badly. There was no two ways about it. A defeat would see Cooper in no man's land – a land that would be hard to come back from.

The title bout against Erskine took place at the Harringay Arena, Harringay, London. Erskine had won the vacant crown on 27th August 1956, with a fifteen-round points decision over former title holder and fellow Welshman Johnny Williams.

The venue for the Erskine-Williams contest was Maindy Stadium, Cardiff, Wales. The title at the time was vacant due to Don Cockell's retirement from boxing.

Since his last winning fight against Cooper on 15th November 1955, by way of a ten-round points victory at the Harringay Arena, Harringay, London, Erskine had entered the ring to ply his trade on six occasions, winning five and losing one.

His resumé now stood at thirty-two bouts, winning thirty, losing one, with one draw. The sole loss came compliments of Cuban-born Nino Valdes, who knocked Erskine out in the first stanza of a scheduled ten. This contest was staged at Earl's Court Arena, Kensington, London, on 19th February 1957. The fight had taken place on the card which saw Cooper's ill-fated attempt to win the Commonwealth crown from Joe Bygraves. The defeat against Valdes did not indicate a weakness in Erskine or a decline in his abilities in any way whatsoever. The Cuban was one tough competitor who could really whack, and he was always dangerous to go up against. It was always a risk to share the ring with this man; once he landed on an opponent's whiskers, it was all over. It was a case of goodnight and goodbye.

When looking at both Cooper's and Erskine's records, it was apparent that the Welshman had a far better resumé than Cooper. In his previous bout before facing Cooper, Erskine had a runout against Peter Bates, whom he outpointed over twelve rounds on 28th May 1957 at the Doncaster Racecourse, Yorkshire. Erskine was in fine form going into the fight with Cooper, and he looked very confident when stepping through the ropes. The challenger would need to up his game if he were to beat Erskine and take the title. The general feeling was that Cooper would have to go for broke in his championship bid and lay it all on the line if he was to succeed and take the title from Erskine.

Sitting back and being cautious would not cut it against the Welshman. Fireworks were expected from the two combatants, but they didn't occur. This was something of a surprise, considering what was at stake.

When the hostilities got underway, the two men boxed carefully, not over-committing; they, of course, knew each other very well from their previous bout. There were no heart-stopping moments during the contest. It wasn't exactly an epic contest, with one man then the other going on the attack. It was more of a chess game with the two men, perhaps over thinking the fight. Punches needed to be thrown with serious intentions, but this failed to happen. The contest went the full distance of fifteen rounds, after which Erskine was declared the victor on points.

This was the first time that Cooper had gone this distance in a contest. Cooper had now lost four bouts in succession. This was not a good look for his boxing career. Realistically, it looked all over for Cooper. Where would he go from here? That was anyone's guess.

When he started out in boxing, he looked to have the ability to go far, to be at least the British and Commonwealth champion one day, or perhaps even a European title holder. Now, it looked like all those grand plans were well and truly dashed. A pessimistic view would be that he had come to the end of the line. It looked as if Cooper would join the ranks of the many hopefuls of the past who had failed to make the grade and fell by the wayside, never to be heard of again. It was a depressing thought, but one which was very much on the mind of many followers of the sport. It would take a great deal of work and planning to turn the situation around for Cooper. But then, it seemed an impossible task.

Jack the First

The challenge of Henry Cooper for Joe Erskine's British heavyweight titles was promoted by Jack Solomons. Thus Solomons became the first man to promote Cooper in a contest for the domestic crown.

Chapter Five
Cooper's Redemption

A Contest in Germany

It may have seemed that Henry Cooper had run out of road. After four defeats on the bounce, he looked to be on a fast train going nowhere. To say the least, the future looked very dismal for him. It all looked like a lost cause, and the party appeared to be over for the British fighter.

However, Cooper and his camp had a different view on the situation: they may well have lost a few battles along the way, but they hadn't lost the war. Their attitude had to be admired. They were not accepting that this was the end of the Cooper story.

The rebuilding process started in Germany on 16th November 1957, when he was matched with home fighter Hans Kalbfell at the Westfalenhalle, Dortmund, Nordrhein-Westfalen. Kalbfell had fought on twenty-one occasions, winning eighteen and losing three.

In his last bout, which took place on the 14th September 1951, Kalbfell won the German heavyweight title when he stopped defending champion Heinz Neuhaus in round eight of twelve, the venue for the bout being where he was now to meet Cooper.

It is always a risk fighting away from home in the opponent's country, as the visitor is given few – if any – favours, a fact which is well documented by events that have taken place in the past. Cooper really couldn't afford to lose another fight. A victory in this outing was vital for him. In fact, it was imperative that he leave the ring a winner. This must have put a great deal of pressure on Cooper when he made his way to the battleground to meet his German opponent. If he did feel the pressure, he didn't show it. He went about the task in front of him in a calm way.

After ten rounds of boxing, Cooper put any fears of another defeat to rest when he controlled the bout using his jab to good effect to rack up a points victory. Cooper was on form, and at no point did he look to be in trouble. He showed that he was a class above the man he was exchanging punches with. This was not a win that would get the top-ranked heavyweights shaking in their boots or running for cover and fearing his name. Truth be told, the victory meant very little on the world stage. It wasn't exactly a headline grabber. To put it in perspective, the victory was only a ripple in a very small pond, but it was a start, an important start, and a ripple can often turn into a wave.

It must be said that at that moment in time, Cooper was not concerned about the rated fighters above him or their opinion of him. He was more concerned with recovering lost ground, career-wise. He knew that he would have to work his way back into contention. There was still a great deal of work to do before he would be taken seriously and have his name linked with the mainstream fighters in the division.

First Draw

It was back to Germany on 11th January 1958, where Henry Cooper hoped to continue to rebuild his career. His last win over Hans Kalbfell was a step in the right direction, but he had to keep the momentum going; that was imperative. He was not out of the woods yet, and he still had much to do.

This time, the opponent coming out of the opposite corner was Heinz Neuhaus – a former European heavyweight champion who came with an impressive resumé of fifty-four bouts, winning forty-one, losing seven, with six drawn. He wasn't exactly wet behind the ears; he was a very experienced fighter.

In his last visit to the ring, Neuhaus had fought fellow countryman Hans Friedrich at the Festhalle, Frankfurt, Hessen, on 12th October 1957, and scored a ten-round points decision over his opponent. The fight against Neuhaus looked to be a much more demanding one than Cooper's last against Kalbfell. The credentials of Neuhaus more than confirmed that he was not going to be a walkover. He clearly didn't come gift-wrapped for Cooper. In short, the German fighter had not turned up to be fodder for Cooper – he was a smart operator and had ambitions of his own. A win over Cooper would serve his boxing career well.

The venue for the Cooper-Neuhaus bout was the Westfalenhalle, Dortmund, Nordrhein-Westfalen. When the bell sounded to start the action, Cooper looked intense when he left his corner. He was well aware that he had to put a win against his name. A defeat against Neuhaus was unthinkable. Cooper boxed well against his opponent – his left jab was eye-catching, landing frequently on target. Cooper looked happy when the fight came to a close, and with good reason. He seemed to have done more than enough to have secured a ten-round points decision. That was not so. The verdict handed down was a draw. The best that could be said about the result is that while it was not a win, it was also not a defeat for the British boxer, and that was a plus to some extent. He was still in the game, hanging on to his career, but only just. This was the first time that Cooper had been in a fight which had resulted in a draw, and for Neuhaus, it was his seventh. So the German was not exactly a stranger to a fight ending in such a fashion.

Third Contest in Germany

Henry Cooper returned to Germany for the third time on 19th April 1958. This time he faced the undefeated Erich Schoppner, who, in his last contest on 22nd February 1958, won the German light-heavyweight title when knocking out holder Willi Hopner in the first round of ten, the venue being Westfalenhalle, Dortmund, Nordrhein-Westfalen. Schoppner's record read twenty-one bouts, with twenty victories, and one draw. That slate suggested that this would not be an easy fight for Cooper, and a win for him was not assured. Schoppner was being touted in Germany as a boxing star of the future.

When facing an opponent with such high expectations in his own country, it was clear Cooper would have to produce something special in the fight to gain the required victory. The venue for the Cooper-Schoppner contest was the Festhalle, Frankfurt, Hessen. Schoppner revealed good skills once the fight began and was giving the British fighter a hard time. His punching was sharp and precise; it was easy to see why he was so highly regarded by his fellow countrymen.

Many of us have had occasions when we felt it just wasn't worth getting out of bed in the morning. This was a thought Cooper might have been having during the course of the battle. The fight against Schoppner was difficult; there was no two ways about that.

At the halfway stage, the German looked as if he had built up a points lead, only a slight one, but nevertheless a lead. There was no great concern in Cooper's corner at that stage. They felt that their man was capable of landing his left hook and hence cancel out any points deficit. The left hook was always a game-changer – once it landed, few opponents were capable of withstanding its force.

However, Cooper wasn't given the opportunity to launch the punch, which might have ended the contest in his favour. In round six of a scheduled ten, he found his name in the loss column. The German fighter hit the deck after taking a solid blow from Cooper, and he stayed there. It looked as if Cooper had put a win on his ledger, but that wasn't the case. The British fighter was disqualified for landing what was considered to be an illegal punch. The Cooper team did not agree with the decision, but the result stood. This was not what the doctor ordered; Cooper was still very much on the sick list, boxing-wise. This was not the result Cooper wanted by far, and was the first and last time that he would suffer a disqualification defeat in his boxing career.

European Light-Heavyweight Champion

On 12th December 1958, in his second fight after defeating Henry Cooper, Erich Schoppner lived up to his potential when he defended his German light-heavyweight crown and also won the European title, defeating fellow countryman Willi Hoepner. The bout took place at the Ernst Merck Halle, Hamburg, Germany. Schoppner captured the title by way of a knockout in round five of a scheduled fifteen. The victory over Hoepner by Schoppner showed that Cooper had shared the ring with a boxer who was not exactly a run-of-the-mill opponent.

Returns to the UK

It could not be overlooked that Henry Cooper's career was still in a precarious position. The defeat against Erich Schoppner did him little, if any, favours for his fistic future. He needed to gain a victory in that fight, and he didn't get it. Cooper badly needed to put another win on his resumé if he was to become relevant again on the domestic scene. The win also needed to be explosive – not one where he went through the motions to snatch a points victory.

On 3rd September 1958, Cooper paid a visit to Wales, and at Coney Beach Arena, Porthcawl, he hoped to make a statement. Cooper stepped in with Welshman Dick Richardson, who had put together a record consisting of thirty-four bouts, winning twenty-five, losing seven, with two drawn.

In his last contest, which took place on 9th July 1958, Richardson had out-pointed Bob Baker from the USA over ten rounds at Coney Beach Arena. Richardson was not an easy touch – far from it: he always came to battle and was not one to surrender meekly to anyone he faced inside the ring. He would throw punches like there was no tomorrow. He didn't hold back. He was a tough man, and with the Welsh supporters giving him every encouragement, he would stride to topple Cooper to ensure that his own future in the fight game was assured. Richardson was the kind of fighter who would push Cooper to the very limits of his ability.

When the bell rang out to start the bout, both men met mid-ring and soon exchanged solid jabs. The Welshman was keen to go to war and quickly closed down the distance between him and his rival. He delivered his own brand of heavy punches, looking to get the upper hand over his opponent. Cooper was more than ready for the advancing Richardson. He used his ramrod jab to pierce the defence of Richardson, rocking him back on his feet.

The Welshman showed little if any concern about the leather thrown in his direction. He had no fear regarding Cooper's power – he kept coming forward, attempting to trap Cooper on the ropes, where he would then thump away to both head and torso. Richardson would take two punches to land one on his opponent. The Welshman had spite in his punches, and he was capable of hurting Cooper, should he land any of them on target.

The fight was shaping up to be a thriller, one where you dare not take your eyes off the ring in case you missed something special. In round five, Richardson found the success he was looking for when he floored his opponent. Cooper didn't look badly hurt, but there was no doubting the fact that this was a critical moment for him. He sensed that the Welshman's success would spur him on to even greater efforts.

On beating the count, Cooper knew that he had to take command of the fight; otherwise, it was not going to end well for him. The Welsh spectators were fully behind their man, willing him on to victory. They felt Richardson was on the brink of winning the bout. At that point, you couldn't argue with their point of view. The Welshman, like his many fans, also felt that this was his moment, and he decided to storm in and finish the job, sending Cooper home a loser.

That was an error in judgment on Richardson's part. Cooper saw his chance and took it – he knew he had the power to end the bout there and then, if he could only detonate the bomb in his left hand, that bomb being the left hook. Cooper found the necessary leverage and the timing: he caught Richardson with the hook as he came in. The Welshman must have felt like he had been hit by a thunderbolt: his body shook and his legs stiffened with the shock of the blow.

The fight was over. Richardson was hurt and in no fit state to carry on. The referee stepped in and made the right call when he stopped the bout. It had been a truly dramatic fifth session. It was a contest that had seen both combatants dig down deep, hoping to find that little extra to take the win. This victory over Richardson was much needed by Cooper to kick-start his career. He was back in the game and more than ready to take the next step in his career.

Richardson Makes History

In his fifth bout after losing to Henry Cooper, Dick Richardson stepped onto German soil on 27th March 1960, to contest the vacant European heavyweight crown. Ingemar Johansson had relinquished the title after winning the world championship from Floyd Patterson on 26th June 1959, by way of a third-round stoppage in a scheduled fifteen at Yankee Stadium, New York, USA. The opponent coming from the opposite corner at the Westfalenhalle, Dortmund, Nordrhein-Westfalen, to face Richardson, was home fighter Hans Kalbfell. Richardson was more than familiar with Kalbfell, since he had previously defeated him on 31st July 1957, by a four-round stoppage in a bout set for ten.

The venue for the Richardson-Kalbfell contest was Coney Beach Arena, Porthcawl, Wales. Both these men had, of course, lost to Henry Cooper in the past. So if you wanted to be cynical, you could ask how on earth the eventual winner of this fight could be regarded as the best in Europe at that poundage, when they had both tasted defeat at the hands of Cooper? It made little or no sense, but then, that's boxing.

Richardson made the most of his opportunity and won the championship when he stopped Kalbfell in round thirteen of fifteen. In winning the title, Richardson put his name in the history books of boxing by becoming the first British boxer to win the European heavyweight championship abroad.

Richardson Does it Again

Dick Richardson returned to Germany on 18th February 1961 to make the second defence of his European heavyweight title against former opponent Hans Kalbfell. (Richardson had made the first defence of the championship against former British & Commonwealth heavyweight king Brian London on 29th August 1960 at Coney Beach Arena, Porthcawl, Wales. Richardson retained the crown when London was halted in round eight of fifteen.)

Richardson was once again victorious when he

successfully retained the European title, out-pointing Kalbfell over fifteen rounds. The Richardson-Kalbfell contest had taken place at the Westfalenhalle, Dortmund, Nordrhein-Westfalen.

In defeating Kalbfell, Richardson made even more history by becoming the first British boxer to have successfully defended this title abroad.

A World Ranked Fighter

Zora Folley from the USA was a world-ranked fighter. He was a class act who had fought quality opposition over the years. His skills inside the ring were admired by many connoisseurs of the sport. He was not a boxer whose ability had faded with the passing of time.

Folley was not playing the role of a stepping stone for Cooper; he was very much in his prime. He was a man with his own ambition of challenging for the heavyweight championship of the world. He hadn't touched down on British soil to lose; that wasn't part of his fight strategy.

So it was somewhat surprising when it was announced that Henry Cooper would meet him in his next contest. One had to wonder why Cooper was taking a bout against a fighter like Folley, who was considered at the time to be the second-best heavyweight in the world after the reigning champion Floyd Patterson, and was on the verge of a title shot. This was a big step up for the British fighter, perhaps a step too far.

The fight looked to be one which would see Cooper defeated – a fight which would reveal his limitations and confirm that he was not yet ready to compete at world level. Folley had amassed an impressive resumé, which consisted of forty-five bouts, winning forty-one, losing two, and drawing two. In his last outing on 25th July 1958, Folley had knocked out Pete Rademacher in round four of ten at the Olympic Auditorium, Los Angeles, California. The American came into the ring at the Empire Pool, Wembley, London, on 14th October 1958, against Cooper, with an air of confidence which radiated around the arena.

In his mind, Folley may well have dismissed Cooper as being a routine exercise – one to keep him punch sharp for bigger fights down the line. To a certain extent, you couldn't blame him if he was thinking this way about his opponent. After all, Folley had met and defeated fighters of a higher calibre than Cooper. Cooper had a demanding fight with Dick Richardson last time out, and Folley was a class above the Welshman. The British fighter, like Folley, had a look of confidence while waiting in his corner for the proceedings to start, but you had to wonder if Cooper's confidence was somewhat misplaced.

Once the bell rang, the two fighters left their respective corners with their hands held high in a defensive position, ready for the action which lay ahead. Their faces were locked in concentration; a great deal was riding on this fight for the pair of them. Folley studied his man carefully, his eyes looking for any weakness which Cooper may have. The American was a craftsman who knew his boxing and would exploit any flaws that his opponent may have.

Cooper probed with his left jab, looking to find a way through Folley's tight defence. The American was well-versed in the tactics Cooper was employing. He showed his quality by moving smoothly away from any possible danger that Cooper may present. One could see almost immediately why Folley was so highly regarded by the boxing pundits in the States. His ring generalship was something to be admired and appreciated. Cooper, despite the challenge he was facing, looked at ease and was not intimidated in any way by the fighter who stood in front of him. This was a good sign, which the ringside spectators quickly picked up on.

There was, however, the constant fear that Cooper's tendency to cut would let him down once his opponent's punches started to fly and land on the tender flesh over his eyes. True enough; the blood manifested itself in the early stages of the contest. The spectators who came to give the British fighter every support were crestfallen at the damage Cooper had sustained. Cooper was cut above and below the left eye. This was concerning; the claret started to run freely down his face. It looked like this could be the beginning of the end for Cooper.

He was in further trouble when Folley put him on the deck in round three for a count with a right hand. The American had some power in his mitts, which Cooper found out to his cost. He looked towards his corner before getting back to his feet to continue the battle. Cooper showed heart as he swapped punches with Folley.

Despite the brave showing, he appeared to be on borrowed time, as he was clearly hurt. At that stage, Cooper looked finished, with no way back. Folley looked to be on the verge of victory, and an early night seemed to be in store for him. Surprisingly, he was unable to close the deal. Cooper had appeared more than ready to be taken out at that time.

One more well-placed left hook or right cross by Folley, and that would have been it: job done, time to go home. It was a rough moment for Cooper. However, he defied the American's attempts to finish him off. He recovered and fought back. It still looked touch-and-go for Cooper at times, but it was noticeable that he was starting to get the upper hand over the American as the fight progressed. It was heartening to see a blood-splattered Cooper rally back after being badly shaken by his opponent. He was still very much in the fight.

The crowd got behind Cooper, giving him every encouragement. He was matching Folly punch for punch. The thudding sound of their heavy blows could be heard at ringside, as both fighters successfully landed their solid punches. Droplets of blood and sweat filled the air as they battled for victory. The contest was exciting: the fans were not only getting a night to remember, but also value for their money. It began to look as if Cooper just might pull it off and score a win over the American. He just had to keep his eye on the ball, stay focused and not make any defensive mistakes; the fight was close, very close. It was not easy to determine who was in front on the scorecard of the referee at the halfway stage of the bout. It was extremely difficult to separate them at that juncture. The two fighters fought tooth and nail, both refusing to give ground in the rounds which followed. Both boxers started to look a little worse for wear, which wasn't surprising, considering the effort they had put in throughout the contest.

In the final stanza, Cooper realised that he had to go for it and dug down deep, throwing everything he had at the American, relentlessly out-punching him until the final second of the ten round fight. At the sound of the bell to end the bout, Cooper hoped that he had done enough to secure the win. Much to his delight, his hand was raised in victory by the referee. The verdict more than pleased the fans, who had come to support him on the night. This, make no mistake, was an outstanding win by Cooper, his best since he'd turned professional. It was a victory which also gave British boxing a much-needed boost. It was an unwanted truth that at the time Britain was the poor relation when it came to producing heavyweights who were considered genuine contenders for the world crown.

Cooper was now highly world-ranked, and what seemed almost impossible to imagine some months ago – a world title shot – was now within his sights. Cooper had now arrived on the big stage, and he was able to share a table with the big boys in the division. He was now considered a name to contend with, a fighter not to be taken lightly. A Brit who just might become a major threat in the heavyweight poundage.

Folley Defeats Bygraves

After the setback against Henry Cooper, Zora Folley fought once again in the UK against former Commonwealth heavyweight king Joe Bygraves at the Granby Halls, Leicester, Leicestershire, in a bout which took place on 24th November 1958. Another defeat was unthinkable for the American. He could not afford a second successive loss on his resumé. Any such fears of being defeated by Bygraves were put to rest when Folley scored a nine-round stoppage in a bout set for ten.

While Folley was pleased to have achieved a victory over Bygraves, it offered him very little in the way of consolation over his loss to Cooper, which had cost him dearly in terms of his world ranking. The defeat to Cooper had been a massive setback for the American, since any immediate plans he may have had for a crack at the championship had all but vanished with that loss. Folley now had to rebuild his fistic career, which would be a painstaking task, but the victory over Bygraves was a start.

First from the USA

The contest with Zora Folley was Henry Cooper's twenty-fifth bout and his first against a fighter from the USA. There were easier opponents from the states whom Cooper could have shared the ring with at that time.

However, Folley was the man brought in to fight Cooper. I suppose one could say it was a gamble, taking on a fighter of Folley's class; one which could have backfired and gone very wrong for Cooper, but when looking at the outcome, it was a gamble that more than paid off for him.

Chapter Six

British and Commonwealth Heavyweight Champion

Cooper Defeats London

12th January 1959 was the big moment for Henry Cooper – a date he would always remember. This was the occasion he secured a second crack at the British and Commonwealth heavyweight title. The reigning champion was Brian London, who was going to be a hard man to beat. After his failure to win the title from Joe Erskine on 17th September 1957 at the Harringay Arena, Harringay, London, by way of a fifteen-round points decision, Cooper had worked his way back into contention, overcoming a host of setbacks to get into the position he was now in. The setbacks he endured would have tempted many fighters to hang up their gloves and consider another profession, but Cooper stuck at it and battled on.

This time around, Cooper was determined to capture the titles, and then move forward with his career, taking the opportunity to be involved in bigger fights in the future. He was now ranked highly in the world following his tremendous victory over the much-touted American Zora Folley, which really put him on the international map. While he must have been feeling over the moon with the win, he could not afford to be complacent against London, and feel that he was going to walk through him. That would be a big mistake. When on form, London was a difficult night's work for anyone. He certainly was not going to surrender the crown to Cooper without a fight – the titles meant a great deal to him. Cooper was more than aware of this fact.

He came prepared for a tough and demanding night against the defending champion. Nothing in life comes easy, and that also goes for winning a championship. The title challenge against London took place at the Earl's Court Arena, Kensington. London. The champion was a man whom Cooper had previously defeated in the opening round in their first meeting, which took place at the Earl's Court Empress Hall, Kensington, London, on 1st May1956. Since that loss to Cooper, London had entered the ring a further twelve times, whereupon he won ten and lost two of his bouts, bringing his resumé up to twenty-five fights with two defeats. This was London's first defence of the titles, which he had taken in impressive style when he knocked out Joe Erskine in round eight of fifteen on 3rd June 1958 at White City Stadium, White City, London.

While Cooper may have easily disposed of London in their previous contest, it was not a foregone conclusion that he would do so again. Time had moved on, and the two men were now much more experienced. The defending champion had first-hand knowledge of the danger his challenger's left hook possessed. He did not want to taste that power again, since it had left a nasty memory; one that lingered long after the fight was over. London clearly didn't want to revisit that painful memory. He felt that this time around, he would beat Cooper and retain the titles. He was itching big time for revenge, and this gave him a great deal of motivation to succeed. He really had no intention of going down in defeat in his first defence of the titles. In his last bout, London had stopped American Willie Pastrano, a future world light-heavyweight champion, by way of a cut-eye stoppage in the fifth stanza of ten at Harringay Arena, Harringay, London, on 30th September 1958.

At the opening bell, Cooper left his corner and went about his task with relish, his left jab constantly landing with considerable force, knocking London back on his heels. The champion, being a consummate professional, responded in kind. The fight was scheduled for fifteen rounds, and many of the spectators speculated whether the contest between two heavy hitters like Cooper and London would go that distance. London was not going to hand over the titles without a fight.

To his credit, he fought back with everything he had in his armoury. The champion was resolute, meeting fire with fire, but it was not enough to defuse the attacking Cooper. The challenger pushed forward, looking for the payoff punch – the punch which would put the title holder to sleep. London was able to withstand the pressure Cooper was applying, but he was consistently picked off and outpunched by him. London refused to back off. He stood his ground and fired back. London had to be admired for his fortitude and resilience. The two men exchanged punches in the centre of the ring. Both fighters were feeling the weight of each other's punches.

It was a brutal, uncompromising battle between the two gladiators. The bruised and swollen features of both champion and challenger were a testament to the punishing encounter which was taking place. Boxing is often called the pain game, and these two fighters were suffering in the ring that night. It was the kind of bout which would take a great deal out of both men. The fighters were giving the cheering spectators a thrilling encounter. Many fans of the sport knew in advance that this was going to be a good fight. Heavyweight bouts, often broadcast from the USA and televised on UK television screens, were always action-packed, giving the spectators a thrilling night of boxing. The Cooper and London bout was a slugfest that more than equalled those epics from across the pond.

At the end of round fourteen, London held Cooper's hand aloft, admitting defeat, seemingly thinking it was the fifteenth and final stanza. It must have been a mental blow for him when he went back to his corner to learn that he had yet another round to go before the final bell. That must have been a nightmare he could have done without. Another three minutes of hard fighting awaited him, with the two men looking worse for wear when they came out to resumé their battle. That was hardly surprising considering what had gone before.

There was no doubt that in the weeks that followed, the two fighters would feel the aches and pains in their bodies every time they moved a muscle. Their fitness in the contest could not be faulted; it was clear the pair had trained long and hard for the fight. At the end of the contest, it was hardly a shock when Cooper was declared the new champion with a points verdict. It was a dream come true for Cooper. It had been a long and hard road to the top, but, finally, he had reached his desired destination. The newly-crowned title holder acknowledged the applause from the spectators. Both Cooper and London had facial damage – a confirmation that it had been a difficult and bitter battle with no quarter given. The new titles would open doors for Cooper in the future. The European crown looked to be on the agenda and well within his reach.

Father and Son

When taking the British and Commonwealth heavyweight titles from Brian London, Henry Cooper defeated a boxer who held a unique record in the sport. Brian's father, Jack London had held the same titles, and hence became the first father and son to do so. London Snr. entered the ring on 15th September 1944 to face Freddie Mills for the vacant titles, which had been relinquished by Len Harvey. London and Mills met at the King's Hall, Belle Vue, Manchester, Lancashire. London thus won the contest when outpointing Mills over the duration of fifteen rounds to secure the titles.

Brian London's Shot at World Title

Despite his defeat to Henry Cooper, Brian London challenged in his very next contest for the world heavyweight title, in a bout which took place on 1st May 1959, against reigning champion Floyd Patterson. The defence against Cooper would be Patterson's fourth. The chances of a London victory weren't very likely. He showed in his bout with Henry Cooper, when losing his British and Commonwealth titles, that he was a tough competitor, but that attribute wouldn't be enough to dethrone a boxer like Patterson, who had a great deal of ring savvy. Saying that, no one could blame London for taking this chance. Fighting for the world title was a big opportunity, one which he really couldn't walk away from, despite the odds being very much against him.

Letting the imagination run wild for a moment, should London emerge victorious, a world title defence against Henry Cooper would be a natural, and something very special, with two Britons contesting the world heavyweight title in the UK. Back to the harsh world of reality, the championship fight between Patterson and London took place at the Fairgrounds Coliseum, Indianapolis, Indiana, USA. London was the first Briton to challenge for the title in the States since Don Cockell, who challenged Rocky Marciano for the championship on 16th May 1955 at the Kezar Stadium, San Francisco, California.

The end for Cockell came in the ninth stanza of fifteen, when the referee stopped the bout in favour of the champion. It had been a painful night. The title attempt by London, as many expected, proved futile: he was knocked out in round eleven of fifteen. The UK would have to continue their wait for a British fighter to come along with the necessary skill set to deliver the world heavyweight title.

Defence of Commonwealth Title

Cooper made the first defence of the Commonwealth heavyweight title on 26th August 1959, against South African heavyweight champion Gawie de Klerk. The venue for the contest was Coney Beach Arena, Porthcawl, Wales. The challenger came with a resumé of nineteen bouts, winning sixteen, and losing three. This was a reasonably good record. In his last bout, de Klerk had out-pointed Italian Domenico Baccheschi over ten rounds at the Rand Stadium, Johannesburg, Gauteng, South Africa, on 9th May 1959. So he was more than ready to take on the British fighter. A win would increase his value greatly on the boxing front. The fight against Cooper would be de Kerk's second bout in the UK.

In his first outing in Britain, he met Peter Bates on 15th April 1958 at the Harringay Arena, Harringay, London, and came away with an eight-round points victory. There was little on the record to suggest that de Klerk would give Cooper any surprises during the contest. After defeating the likes of Zora Folley and Brian London, de Klerk was considered to be a routine bout, not one which could be called challenging. The general opinion was that Cooper would enter the ring as the champion and leave it as the champion. There would be no changing of the guard on the night. The last South African-born holder of the Commonwealth title was Ben Foord, who reigned from 17th August 1936 to 15th March 1937.

After his hard-fought victory over Brian London, whereupon he won the British and Commonwealth titles, Cooper was on the crest of a wave. The battle with London had drawn great praise from fans and critics alike. Cooper was keen to keep the momentum going and make a big impression against de Klerk. He was buzzing going into the ring, and he wanted to show that he was a champion of substance – one who would reign for some considerable time. The spectators at ringside sat back in their seats, anticipating a good night of boxing with fireworks.

However, there was not a great deal of action in the early stages of the scheduled fifteen-round contest, which was a little disappointing for the fans who wanted to see the fighters get stuck in and slug it out. The two boxers appeared to be cautious of each other, neither one of them wanting to make a mistake. Cooper pushed out his left jab, attempting to find his range. It looked as if the fight would go into the later stages, but then his left hook came into play, and that changed everything: the punch landed with explosive force, which ended the proceedings in the fifth session.

The referee halted the bout after the South African rose from the canvas after being dropped by the champion for a second time in that stanza. He was clearly in no state to continue, so the stoppage was a good call. The evening was over for de Klerk. South Africa was not claiming the Commonwealth crown on this night.

Gawie de Klerk Bids Farewell to Boxing

After his failure to take the Commonwealth title from Henry Cooper, Gawie de Klerk indulged in a further ten fights, of which he won eight and lost two. De Klerk participated in his last professional bout on 7th October 1961, at the Speedway Stadium, Pretoria, Gauteng, South Africa. On this outing, de Klerk defeated his opponent, Ewald Stanke, who retired in round two of a contest scheduled for eight. During his professional career, Gawie de Klerk took part in thirty bouts, of which he won twenty-four and lost six.

Last South African Challenger

The last boxer from South Africa to challenge for the Commonwealth heavyweight title before Gawie de Klerk was Johnny Arthur, who had two bites of the apple. His first bid for the crown came on 13th October 1952, against Johnny Williams. Arthur was defeated when he retired in round seven of fifteen. The venue for the Williams-Arthur title contest was Granby Halls, Leicester, Leicestershire.

The second and final challenge for the Commonwealth crown by Arthur took place on 30th January 1954, against the then champion Don Cockell of England. On this occasion, Arthur had home advantage, so the South African fans were optimistic about his chances of taking the crown from Cockell. The fight took place at Rand Stadium, Johannesburg, Gauteng. It went the full distance of fifteen rounds. Once again, Arthur failed in his bid when Cockell retained the crown by way of points decision.

Cooper and Erskine Meet Again

Duty called again on 17th November 1959, when Henry Cooper walked into the ring at Earl's Court Arena, Kensington, London, to defend his British and Commonwealth heavyweight titles against an opponent with whom he was more than familiar. That man was former champion Joe Erskine. This was a rival whom Cooper had lost to on two previous occasions in the paid ranks. Erskine was confident that he had Cooper's number and would once again get the better of him, and in so doing, regain the titles he once proudly held.

Cooper had other ideas. He was set on getting revenge for the defeats he had suffered against Erskine. Cooper did not doubt that he would leave the ring still holding the titles at the end of their meeting. The Welshman did represent a risk. There could be no argument – he was a clever boxer, as Cooper well knew from his past experiences when boxing him. Erskine could not be written off without a chance. In his last outing, which took place on 26th August 1959, Erskine had out-pointed Italian heavyweight title holder Bruno Scarabellin over ten rounds at the Coney Beach Arena, Porthcawl, Wales. His resumé now stood at forty bouts, consisting of thirty-six wins, three defeats and one draw.

The two fighters embraced the applause from the spectators in the arena as they stepped into the ring. The fans were looking forward to a good night's boxing from the two men. They were not going to be disappointed. When the fight started, Cooper was at his most destructive. He was determined that the fight would not go the full distance of fifteen rounds. Cooper hunted his man down, landing with spiteful punches which took their toll on Erskine. The Welshman did well to take the blows, which hit him squarely to both head and body. There was no disputing that the Welshman had more than his fair share of courage to complement his boxing skills, but the end of his challenge was in sight.

Erskine was slowing down; the stream of jabs, mixed with the left hook of Cooper, was draining the strength from his challenger bit by bit. Erskine was now finding it difficult to fend off the attacking Cooper. His legs lacked the movement they previously had in the early rounds. The distress signals were being read loud and clear by Cooper, who knew his man was ready for the taking. The champion finally put a finish to Erskine's bid to regain the titles when his left hook devastatingly found its target, in round twelve of fifteen. The referee stopped the bout with the Welshman lying dramatically on the bottom rope. Erskine's night was well and truly over. It was a breathtaking finish by Cooper. The image of Erskine's unconscious state remained in the minds of many people after the contest was over. It was further confirmation of the power Cooper had in his left hook. Cooper had well and truly avenged the defeats he had suffered against Erskine in the past.

Married

Henry Cooper first met his future wife, Italian-born Albina Genepri, at a restaurant called Peter Mario's in Gerrard Street, London, where she was working. He took his time, but he eventually asked her to go out with him. Much to his pleasure, Albina accepted his invitation. In 1960, a happy event took place when the couple were married. In the fullness of time, the happy couple were blessed with the birth of two sons, Henry Marco and John Pietro.

Cooper Defeats a Former World Title Challenger

Roy Harris from the USA was the next man to share the ring with Henry Cooper, in a bout which took place on 13th September 1960. Harris was a decent enough opponent for Cooper to face at this stage of his career. He had compiled a slate of thirty-three bouts, which saw him victorious in twenty-nine bouts, with three defeats, and one no contest. Harris had fought quality fighters in the past, perhaps not always achieving the best of results in so doing, but he had, at least, faced them, which said something about his fighting character and experience. Harris had challenged Floyd Patterson on 18th August 1958 for the world heavyweight crown, failing in his bid when he retired in round twelve of fifteen at Wrigley Field, Los Angeles, California.

The defeat against Patterson did not dishearten Harris – he continued with his career. He still had ambition and hoped that he might be able to get another title opportunity should he put some more victories on his record. All such hopes came to a finish when, in his seventh bout after the Patterson loss, he faced future world heavyweight king Sonny Liston on 25th April 1960. The venue for the meeting with Liston was the Sam Houston Coliseum, Houston, Texas, where he was dispatched unceremoniously in the opening session of a scheduled ten-round contest by the heavy-hitting Liston.

Then, on 27th July 1960, he entered the ring once more, hoping to get a much-needed win, but he was unable to achieve the desired result; he was knocked out by Canadian Bob Cleroux in the fifth stanza of a contest slated for the duration of ten rounds. The Harris-Cleroux bout took place at the Delormier Stadium, Montreal, Quebec, Canada. This meant Harris was coming into the ring at the Empire Pool, Wembley, London, to face Cooper with two successive inside-the-distance defeats behind him. This did not bode well for his chances against Cooper, who, of course, could bang a bit with his left hook.

So it was hoped that Cooper might emulate Liston and Cleroux, and win before the final bell sounded. The spectators' eyes were firmly fixed on the ring, not wanting to miss any second of the action which was about to unfold. Cooper started smartly, taking command with his educated left jab. Cooper also landed some powerful shots but was unable to put his man away. Harris was able to absorb the punches which Cooper delivered and see the fight out to the final bell. Cooper may have been unable to stop his man, but on the plus side, the British fighter did put in a good, solid performance to take the verdict. He boxed well, winning by way of a ten-round points decision. True, a stoppage victory by Cooper would have been more preferable, but a win is a win, and that is what counts in the sport. Cooper could now move on to his next objective.

Chapter Seven

Folley Defeats Cooper

Cassius Clay Makes His Debut

On 29th October 1960, a contest took place at the Freedom Hall, Louisville, Kentucky, USA. Tunney Hunsaker lost a six-round points decision to an opponent who was making his professional debut.

In the fullness of time, the winning boxer would prove to be very relevant to the career of Henry Cooper and to the world of boxing. His name was Cassius Clay, a former Olympic gold medallist at light-heavyweight, winning said medal at the 1960 games, which were held in Rome, Italy. To take the desired medal, Clay defeated Poland's Zbigniew Pietrzykowski on points over three rounds in the final. Clay later changed his name to Muhammad Ali, a fighter who was destined to join the greats in the division.

The Man from Argentina

It was time for Henry Cooper to slip on the gloves once again and get back into the ring. His opponent this time around was Argentinian-born Alex Miteff, who arrived with a resumé of twenty-nine bouts, winning twenty-two, losing six, with one drawn. He was no soft touch. He knew his way around the ring, so Cooper could not afford to underestimate this man. In his previous contest, Miteff had lost a ten-round contest to Eddie Machen by way of a points decision on 20th May 1960.

The bout against Machen had taken place at Madison Square Garden, New York. That defeat was nothing to be ashamed of. Machen was a class act, who was not easy to overcome.

On this night, he was capable of upsetting anyone who came out of the opposite corner. During his time trading punches, Machen had duelled with the best in the division. It must be said that had Machen faced Cooper, he would have been a severe test for Cooper.

Cooper stepped into the ring to meet Miteff on 6th December 1960, the venue being the Empire Pool, Wembley, London. It was the festive month, but Miteff had not come to the UK bearing gifts for Cooper – he had no intention of playing the role of Santa Claus or spreading joy and good tidings towards the British fighter. His mind was focused on putting a loss on Cooper's record before returning home. He didn't arrive on British shores to enhance Cooper's reputation. That was not part of his overall plan. It was no secret that Cooper held no fears for him. Miteff knew how to use the gloves, and he intended to put them to good use in this fight. The man from Argentina was one tough hombre, that was apparent. He clearly held the view that he had shared the ring with better opposition than Cooper and would dispose of him without too much difficulty. When the fight started, there was a feeling of tension in the air. There was something about Miteff which was a little unsettling. His demeanour before the opening bell was one of confidence. He didn't look like a man who would submit easily.

Once the bout started, Cooper fought well and was in control of the fight, picking his punches well. He was in good form, looking very sharp and composed. The rounds slipped by with Cooper maintaining his control over the man in front of him. He took the occasional jab from Miteff, which jolted his head back. That was nothing to be alarmed about – that's boxing, you hit and get hit. That was the nature of the sport. You can't take a shower without getting wet.

Despite this, Cooper looked home and dry – on his way to a good victory, until the tenth stanza arrived; this round was almost a disaster for him. Miteff, who still looked strong, dug down – and very much against the run of play – floored Cooper, who crashed to the canvas heavily. The situation did not look good for Cooper. He beat the referee's count and arose on unsteady legs at the count of nine. The British fighter was badly hurt – that was obvious to the spectators, and to Miteff, who was now close to sending Cooper home a loser. The Argentinian would now come with all guns blazing for the home fighter, with every intention of blasting him into unconsciousness.

These were anxious moments for Cooper, as Miteff pushed forward on the attack. He was relentless and felt with good reason that he was going to grab victory from the very jaws of defeat. It was an amazing turnaround for the Argentinian, who was a man who clearly could not be written off. Cooper was glassy-eyed, but showed a fighter's heart and bravely managed to hold on until the bell rang to end the ten round bout. The sound of that bell must have sounded like sweet music to the ears of the British fighter and to his many supporters, who must have feared the worst for him.

A bloodied Cooper was given the decision on points, but he was aware that it had been a close call. He almost had an unexpected loss added to his record. That was something he really didn't need at this stage, and one which would clearly have ruined his Christmas.

Wins Lonsdale Belt Outright

Henry Cooper stepped into the ring once again on 21st March 1961 at the Empire Pool, Wembley, London, to defend the British and Commonwealth heavyweight titles against his old adversary Joe Erskine. Cooper needed to shine in this outing. He was badly shaken up in his last bout against Alex Miteff and looked on the verge of defeat against the Argentinian, so he needed to be on top form against the Welshman.

Since they had last crossed gloves, Erskine had participated in two winning contests, which had taken his resumé to forty-three bouts, consisting of thirty-eight wins, four defeats, with one draw. In his last bout, which had taken place on 24th January 1961, Erskine had boxed Ulli Ritter of Germany at Granby Halls, Leicester, Leicestershire, winning a solid ten-round points decision. At the commencement of his title contest against Cooper, Erskine started confidently. He exchanged left jabs with the champion.

The two boxers were business-like as they went about their work. The spectators, as per usual, waited in anticipation for Cooper's left hook to land. Erskine was not noted for being a big puncher, but he was a good boxer, with skills that were envied by many in the fight game. He moved well around the square circle, evading the champion's heavy shots with clever head movement.

However, Cooper was watching his man like a hawk, anticipating Erskine's next move. He started to cut down the ring and gradually increased the tempo of the fight, catching the Welshman with his solid jabs, which were clearly affecting him. The fight was scheduled for fifteen rounds, but came to its conclusion in the fifth, when Erskine was halted with a badly damaged left eye. There were no exciting highlights during the contest, no edge-of-your-seat drama. The contest was not exactly a barn burner; the fight lacked fire. The bout promised much, but delivered very little in the way of thrilling action. Cooper got the job done, and that was the important thing. Cooper not only retained the titles but won the Lonsdale Belt outright for achieving three British championship victories. The belt was his for keeps. He could now put it on display in his trophy cupboard. It was a proud token of all the hard work and endurance he had put into the sport.

All in all, it was a good night's work for Cooper, who could now push on with his career and look towards bigger fights in the foreseeable future.

Folley's Revenge

When they had previously met on 14th October 1958, Henry Cooper secured a ten-round points victory over Zora Folley of the USA at the Empire Pool, Wembley, London.

At the time, it was seen to be the best win of Cooper's professional career, one that had greatly elevated his position in world boxing, making him a name on the big stage. A name to respect and beware of, a Briton who looked capable of shaking things up amongst the big guns in the division.

Now the pair were back at the Empire Pool to exchange leather once again. Since their last meeting, Folley had been very active, fighting on sixteen occasions, winning fourteen, and losing two. This brought his resumé up to sixty-two bouts, consisting of fifty-five victories, five defeats, with two draws.

Folley, in his previous contest, had out-pointed Sonny Moore over ten rounds in a bout that took place on 28th September 1961. The venue for the Folley-Moore contest was the County Coliseum, El Pasco, Texas. Moore had been around in his day and was by no means a novice to the sport, but if truth be told, he was not in Folley's class. So the win proved little, if anything at all. Frankly, the result hardly stunned the followers of boxing. No one in the fight game stood back in awe when hearing the result. The contest merely provided Folley with a workout, giving him some rounds and punch practice, before stepping in with Cooper for a second time.

It was felt that Cooper would score the double over Folley. It would not be easy, but it certainly wasn't beyond his capabilities to do so – what Cooper did once, he could do again, was the understandable reasoning. A second victory over Folley would see the home fighter in with a great chance of having a shot at the world crown. Sadly, for Cooper, that was not to be the case. In hindsight, it may have been wiser to have avoided the return with Folley, but as we all know, hindsight is a wonderful thing.

On 5th December 1961, Folley entered the roped arena

against Cooper. A determined Folley gained his revenge when he knocked out the British fighter in the second round of ten. Folley executed the blow with the kind of expertise you would expect from a world-class fighter. Cooper fell face down onto the canvas. There would be no coming back from such a punch – his night was well and truly over. This was a devastating defeat for Cooper. Folley had looked the more dominant fighter from the opening bell.

The American was sharp and took out Cooper with ease. Cooper wasn't able to get going. He was simply wiped out by the American. Folley was not troubled at all by Cooper during the short time the fight lasted. It was an easy night for the visitor from the USA, a very easy payday for him. No one felt that the fight would end the way it did, or indeed as quickly as it did. Those in attendance were taken aback by the nature of Cooper's quick defeat. Folley showed that he had the kind of power in his punches that more than equalled the power of Cooper's left hook. The American departed from the ring that night a satisfied man with a job well done. In his mind, he had set the record straight.

There would be no third meeting between the two fighters. This was a setback for Cooper, make no mistake. One which he could ill afford at this stage of his career. Cooper had to come to terms with this defeat; he had no choice but to do so. These things happen in boxing, and to his credit, Cooper had shown before that he had the resilience to bounce back from defeat, and there was every indication that he would do so again. The party wasn't over yet.

Folley's World Title Chance

After defeating Henry Cooper, Zora Folley looked to be

heading for a shot at the world crown. If he was waiting for a phone call to be given the news of such an event, he had a very long wait. He was given his world title chance twenty-three fights later, the time period for the occasion being an amazing five years, three months and seventeen days. His long-overdue opportunity took place against the reigning world heavyweight king, Muhammad Ali, on 22nd March 1967 at Madison Square Garden, New York. No one felt that Folley would take the title from Ali. As expected, Folley failed in his bid when knocked out in round seven of fifteen. Ali won without any kind of difficulty over his opponent.

Truthfully, it was an easy outing for the undefeated champion, who just went through the gears. Folley was way past his best when his opportunity to go for the championship eventually arrived. Perhaps had his chance come earlier in his career, he might have won the title, who knows? When his chance finally arrived, it was against a man of exceptional talent in the shape of Ali. It appeared that the boxing fates were not on Folley's side.

Cooper Back on Winning Trail

Henry Cooper returned to action on 23rd January 1962 at the Empire Pool, Wembley, London. He had to put the nightmare defeat against Zora Folley to one side and concentrate on the job in hand. What was done was done. Cooper couldn't change the past; he now had to look to the future, with the mindset of getting back on the victory trail.

The opponent coming out of the opposite corner was Tony Hughes of the USA, who arrived with a resumé of twenty-five bouts, winning twenty–four, with one defeat.

The American's only loss had come in his last contest, when he was out-pointed over ten rounds by fellow countryman Alonzo Johnson on 8th December 1961 at the Civic Arena, Pittsburgh, Pennsylvania.

The record looked good, with there being just that one defeat on Hughes' slate. Yet it was noticeable when taking an intense close look at his resumé, that the opposition he had faced in the past were hardly world beaters. It would, of course, have been foolish to have written Hughes off as a no-hoper. The American was ambitious and had his eyes set on bigger fish in the division.

A win over Cooper would clearly advance his career somewhat. So Hughes had a great deal to gain, should he walk away from the ring with a victory, especially with the contest being on Cooper's own ground. During the course of the fight, there were no challenging moments for Cooper. He was caught with the occasional jab, but nothing too serious. Cooper bossed the fight and looked comfortable. He moved well around the ring, constantly shooting out his left jab, which had some sting in it, a fact the American could testify to.

The ten-round contest came to a close in the fifth session, with the referee intervening due to Hughes having a badly cut eye. The American was brave in defeat, but was out of his depth. There are levels in boxing, and Cooper was on a much higher level than Hughes. Cooper was back to winning and ready to move on to more challenging encounters.

Defeats Bethea

On 26th February 1962, Henry Cooper was gloved up once

more and ready to go to work. His next foray into the ring took place at the King's Hall, Belle Vue, Manchester, Lancashire. His opponent on this occasion was Wayne Bethea, another boxer from the USA.

Bethea had won his last contest, out-pointing fellow countryman Frankie Daniels over eight rounds in Germany on 11th November 1961. The venue for the Bethea-Daniels bout was the Westfalenhalle, Dortmund, Nordrhein-Wesfalen.

During his career, Bethea had accumulated a record consisting of forty-two bouts, winning twenty-four, losing sixteen, with two draws. The American was a competent ring man who had previously met a host of top-calibre fighters in his time, but did not appear to be a threat to Cooper.

However, you cannot take anything for granted in the sport of boxing. One careless moment, one lack of concentration, and bang – it's all over. At that time, Bethea had only been defeated inside the distance on just one occasion. It was Sonny Liston on 6th August 1958 who did the deed, ensuring that Bethea would not hear the final bell. He stopped him in the first round of ten.

The short-lived contest between Liston and Bethea had taken place at the Chicago Stadium, Chicago, Illinois, USA. Not many fighters survived the full distance in a fight once Liston had caught them flush. The man could hit and then some. When leaving his corner to face Bethea, Cooper was sharp and was very much on form. His left jab snaked out, hitting his opponent frequently. Cooper owned the fight, much to the joy of the spectators. Apart from his jab, Cooper stung the American with solid combinations to both head and body, which he clearly felt. To his credit, Bethea was able to shake off the effects of the punches.

Cooper couldn't equal Liston's feat by stopping the American, but truth be told, few boxers could match Liston's power. The contest with Bethea thus went the full ten rounds, of which Cooper emerged victorious with a points decision. You had to give kudos to Bethea for showing his durability against Cooper in the contest. Cooper could now look forward to the future with renewed vigour.

Erskine Again

The Ice Rink, Nottingham, was the next port of call for Henry Cooper, where he defended his British and Commonwealth heavyweight titles. His challenger, and former holder of the titles, was a man Cooper knew so very well – Joe Erskine. The Welshman had fought just once since he last engaged Cooper. That contest took place in Canada, at the Maple Leaf Gardens, Toronto, Ontario, on 2nd October 1961. Erskine took on home fighter George Chuvalo. That was a risky bout for him to take, since the Canadian was a tough pressure fighter.

Chuvalo was always dangerous until the very end, with his never-die approach to his contests. Clearly, in front of his fans, he would be far from easy to beat. It looked as if certain defeat was waiting for the Welshman in Canada.

However… surprise, surprise! Erskine came away with an unexpected win when the home fighter was disqualified in round five of ten. This was a good result for the Welshman, defeating Chuvalo on his own turf. This took some doing, even if by a disqualification. Erskine now had a record of forty-five fights, with thirty-nine victories, five defeats, with one draw. He was more than ready to rumble with Cooper, feeling that he would take the win on this outing and have the title belts strapped around his waist once more.

On 2nd April 1962, the two men came out of their respective corners to do battle. Surprisingly, Erskine looked to be getting the upper hand over Cooper in the early stages of the contest. He boxed well; his footwork was exceptional. His jab was superb; it was both fast and accurate, picking up valuable points when it landed. It had to be wondered if this was going to be Erskine's night, and the titles were on their way back to Wales. Cooper looked a little sluggish and had problems finding his range. He was aware that he would need to get his act together, pick up the pace and take the play away from Erskine if he was to retain the titles. The defending champion pushed forward and eventually took control of the bout.

Cooper was now timing his punches, which landed sufficiently to inflict facial damage on his opponent. Cooper's punches were clearly hurtful; the champion finally turned the tide in his favour and looked to be heading for victory. Erskine was hanging in there, even while he now seemed to be fighting a losing battle. In round nine of fifteen, it was all over when the bout was stopped in Cooper's favour, due to Erskine suffering from a bad cut over his eye, making it impossible for him to continue. While the fight lasted, Erskine put in a more than creditable performance against Cooper.

Three Times in Succession

When Henry Cooper defended the British and Commonwealth heavyweight championship against Joe

Erskine at the Ice Rink, Nottingham on 2nd April 1962, it made history, as it was the first time that the same two boxers had fought three times in succession for these titles.

Erskine's Farewell

After being unsuccessful in his final bid to regain the British and Commonwealth heavyweight titles from Henry Cooper, Erskine took to the ring on eight more occasions. In said bouts, he won six and lost two of the respective contests.

His last outing took place at the Empire Pool, Wembley, London, on 27th October 1964, whereupon he lost a ten-round points decision to Billy Walker – a defeat which convinced him that his time in boxing was over, and it was time to bid farewell to the sport. During his career, Joe Erskine had taken part in fifty-four bouts, of which he won forty-five, lost eight and drew one.

Dick Richardson

After Joe Erskine, another Welshman, the former European heavyweight champion Dick Richardson, climbed between the ropes in an attempt to wrestle the British and Commonwealth heavyweight titles away from Cooper.

The bout between the pair took place on 26th March 1963, at the Empire Pool, Wembley, London. In their last encounter, on 3rd September 1958 at Coney Beach Arena, Porthcawl, Wales, Cooper emerged victorious in a tough fight by stopping Richardson in the fifth round of ten. It was a contest that had been touch-and-go for Cooper. He looked on the edge of defeat before he got out of trouble by landing his left hook.

Since that defeat, Richardson had paid a visit to the ring

on eleven occasions, winning six and losing five. This took his tally to forty-six bouts, consisting of thirty-one wins, thirteen defeats, with two draws. In his last foray into the ring, Richardson had lost his European crown to former world heavyweight king, Ingemar Johansson, on 17th June 1962 by a knockout in round eight of fifteen in a contest that had taken place at Nya Ullevi, Gothenburgh, Sweden. Johansson hence regained the title, which he had relinquished when capturing the world crown from Floyd Patterson. Richardson was confident that, this time around, he had the tools to do the job and take the victory and dethrone Cooper. He was more than ready for a war.

Cooper, as always, trained hard for the bout – he knew what to expect from Richardson and was not taking him lightly. Cooper steeled himself for the storm that was certain to come his way. When the bout commenced, the fighters left their starting blocks quickly, ready to engage. The champion used his left jab, consistently scoring valuable points as the rounds passed by. Each session was filled with drama. Cooper was gradually wearing the Welshman down with his superior boxing skills.

Richardson bit down on his gumshield and tried to walk Cooper down, but he was being punished for his efforts. It was a painful occasion for the challenger. The champion finally dispatched Richardson in round five of a bout scheduled for fifteen. The end was not surprising; Cooper had worn his man down and landed the *coup de grâce* when the time was right. The fight was not easy. Cooper wasn't able to relax for one moment during the contest, and he must have been relieved when the bout was finally over. The Welshman was tough, and he was always looking to land the winning punch.

Richardson Retires from Boxing

The defeat against Henry Cooper was the last time that Dick Richardson would put on the gloves and enter the ring to do battle. He later retired from boxing. During his career, Dick Richardson took part in forty-seven professional contests, of which he won thirty-one, lost fourteen and drew two. He was a fighter who constantly gave his all in the bouts he was involved in and shared the ring with a number of top-line heavyweights.

Chapter Eight
Cooper and Clay Meet

Cassius Clay in the UK

The UK saw the visit of Cassius Clay – a fighter from the USA who was extremely talented – and not backwards in telling all and sundry just how great he was. He had won the gold medal at light-heavyweight at the 1960 Olympic Games, which took place in Rome, Italy, defeating Poland's Zbigniew Pietrzkowski by way of a three-round points decision in the final. Clay was the man Henry Cooper was about to share the ring with – a tough ask for the British fighter, but one he was more than ready to take on.

Upon arriving in the UK, Clay made it known that he was not impressed by Cooper, making light of the home fighter's capabilities. He predicted the round in which their fight would end and how easy it was going to be for him to win the contest, suggesting Cooper was not in his class. It would be correct to say that he did not make many friends with that statement in the UK. The words spoken did not sit well with the public, who did not like to see their man ridiculed in this way.

Throughout it all, Cooper remained calm and realised that Clay's antics were going to help sell tickets, and that was good for the two of them, which in turn meant it was also good for their bank balances. So it was a win-win situation, which sat well with Cooper, so he didn't mind the insults; he could take them all day long. The fight garnered a great deal of attention from the media. It was hot news. The fight had everybody talking – boxing was in the limelight in a big way. The weigh-in for the bout took place at the famous London Palladium, a theatre which, over the years, had seen many top entertainers from all over the world perform there. On the night of 18th June 1963, the two men of contrasting personalities met at Wembley Stadium, Wembley, London.

Clay entered the ring dressed in a purple and gold ankle-length gown with the wording 'Cassius Clay the Greatest' emblazoned on the back of the garment. It was a very eye-catching sight.

On his head, he wore a cardboard crown, which ignited boos from spectators, but this did little to unnerve him. In fact, Clay seemed to enjoy and encourage it; he was the bad guy of the piece, and was milking it for all it was worth.

Cooper entered the ring and was greeted with a rapturous reception from the fans. He wore a blue and white gown with the wording 'Henry Cooper, England' emblazoned on the back of his attire. A modest gown, compared to Clay's. The American was a showman as well as being an excellent boxer – he knew how to sell a fight, and he sold it well. No one could argue with that. He was a top-class salesman.

Going into the contest with Cooper, Clay had an

undefeated resumé, consisting of eighteen fights. In his last bout, which had taken place on 13th March 1963, he out-pointed fellow countryman Doug Jones over ten rounds. Jones gave Clay a demanding night, pushing him hard, which gave the impression that Clay may not be that unbeatable after all. Yet it should not be overlooked that Jones was a good fighter, and anyone meeting him could expect more than their share of problems. A fighter really had to be on his game to beat him. The contest between Jones and Clay had taken place at Madison Square Garden, New York. Clay was not known to be a powerful puncher, but he had won fourteen of his bouts inside the scheduled distance. This signified that he had some sting in his punches.

It was no secret that many hoped that Cooper would put this young upstart in his place, and introduce him to the left hook known as 'Enry's 'Ammer', and send him packing back to the USA with his first professional defeat on his record. Clay wanted to spread the word about his abilities, confirming that he was the genuine article and was no hype job, a sure-fire future world heavyweight champion.

There were a number of celebrities spotted amongst the spectators, including actors Richard Burton and Elizabeth Taylor. This added even more glitter to the event.

Once the bell sounded, Cooper made a fast start, giving his opponent very little breathing space, blocking his avenues of retreat. Cooper even gave Clay a nosebleed within seconds of the battle commencing. This surprised Clay a little. He was not used to this treatment, and he did not like it one little bit. It was looking good for Cooper, but there was still a long way to go in the ten-round contest.

The second stanza saw Cooper continue his good work, but he ended the session with a cut under the left eye, which was a setback, since it was now well-documented that he was prone to cuts. The wound would now be a target for Clay to aim at during the contest. Cooper ignored the cut, occasionally brushing the blood flow away from his eye with his gloved hand, and continued to go forward. He didn't allow the cut to put him off his plan of attack.

In the fourth stanza, a confident Clay danced around Cooper, shooting out a stiff jab, feeling that a victory was within his grasp. He was almost past the winning post. The fight was there for him to win. What could go wrong? Then the unexpected happened, Cooper caught Clay with his left hook. It seemed to come out of nowhere and exploded perfectly on target. The American felt the full force of the blow and, in response, slid down the ropes onto the canvas. His eyes told the story. He was, for a moment, in a dream state. He was, to phrase an old Elvis Presley song, 'All Shook Up'. This was sensational. It was only the second time that Clay had been put on the deck in the professional ranks. The spectators were ecstatic. They roared in appreciation of the punch which Cooper had delivered. Clay was hurt; there was no doubt about that. He looked ready for the taking. It was well-known that Cooper was a good finisher, once he had his man hurt, but the fates were on the side of the American. The bell sounded to end the stanza before Cooper could follow up. Had Cooper connected earlier in the round, there was every chance that he would have stopped Clay and dramatically changed the heavyweight landscape. Sometimes a little luck plays a big hand in how a situation develops in a fight. It looked for a brief moment that Cooper might be on his way to a spectacular win, despite all the odds which were stacked against him.

Clay's corner men managed to contain any panic they may have felt, but they must have seriously been concerned at the sight of their man being clipped on the chin. They knew their charge was hurt, perhaps more hurt than he had ever been before in the paid ranks. The world-renowned trainer, Angelo Dundee, remained calm; he worked tirelessly to bring Clay back to his senses during the interval. Dundee had been around the sport for a long time, and knew all the tricks, and wasn't afraid to put them to use to save his man. Dundee was a craftsman in his trade and quickly got to work, reviving his fighter, getting his head clear, ready to resumé the battle. Dundee was clearly an ace card in Clay's corner.

There was a delay to the following stanza when it was found that Clay's glove was damaged. The delay, no matter how short, was an advantage to the American. Every second would have been vital for his recovery.

When the bell rang to start the fifth round, the two men left their corners with the same purpose. That purpose was not only to win, but to win as quickly as possible. Cooper was looking to follow up on his earlier success and land the payoff punch. Sadly, for him, the window of opportunity for victory had now passed. Clay had now recovered from the blow that had put him on the deck. He was now fully educated about the power Cooper had in his left hook, and he now had more respect for the man he was facing. Clay was no fool; he may not have taken Cooper too seriously before the bout, but he was taking him seriously now. Cooper was dangerous and a threat to his potential world title shot against Sonny Liston. Clay could not allow Cooper to get in his way and wreck his plans. He had to end the fight and get rid of Cooper without any further delay.

This he did when he inflicted more damage to Cooper's eye, which streamed blood down his face like a crimson waterfall. It was not a pretty sight. Not one for the faint-hearted. Even some of the hardened boxing fans, who had seen it all in their time, diverted their eyes for a moment. The referee had no choice but to step in and call a halt to the fight. The bloodied Cooper was both frustrated and dismayed at the stoppage in equal measure. It was a massive disappointment for him. Cooper may have lost the fight, but the knockdown he scored against Clay ensured that his name would be discussed for many years to come whenever the fight was discussed in conversation. It had been an excellent contest, one that lived up to all expectations, and one which would be a talking point for many months to come. The contest had enhanced the British fighter's reputation greatly.

First Time Outside of the USA

The contest with Henry Cooper at Wembley Stadium proved to be one of both excitement and drama. It was interesting to note that this was the first time that Cassius Clay had ventured outside of the USA, in the professional ranks, he stepped into a bout that almost saw him come unstuck.

Conjecture

Many have speculated over the years on what might have happened had Henry Cooper's left hook struck earlier during the fourth round, thus giving Cooper more time to finish Cassius Clay. Had Cooper been able to stop the American, it would have delayed any potential plans he and his management team may have had for challenging Sonny Liston for the world heavyweight title. Cooper might have moved into the position of world title challenger.

In boxing, decisions have to be made by the boxer's manager with caution; they must tread carefully when planning their charge's next move. The shrewd Jim Wicks, the manager of Cooper, was a clever man and knew the fight game well. He had years of experience behind him in the sport and had learned a great deal from working with various fighters. Wicks might very well have taken the view that Liston was all wrong for Cooper. The world champion was a brutal puncher and would have certainly cut Cooper badly with his powerful punches, if not knock him out. The fight would not have lasted too long, that was for certain.

This is, of course, speculation. The chances are that a return contest with Clay would have been arranged, since the American would have badly wanted to avenge the defeat against Cooper and get his career back on track. When looking at the two options presented, the return with Clay would have looked to have been the most likely for Cooper, rather than entering the ring to face a man like Liston, even if it was for the world title.

First Promoter to Bring Clay to the UK

The Henry Cooper and Cassius Clay contest was one big event. It really galvanised boxing in Britain. Matching Clay, the latest heavyweight hotshot from the USA, against Cooper was a good move by both promoters and management. Cooper was a firm favourite with the home fans. So the bout really caught the imagination of the fight fraternity. The promotion was put together by Jack Solomons, who can claim to be the first promoter to bring Clay to the UK shores and indeed Europe.

Jack Solomons Awarded

In 1978, Jack Solomons was awarded an OBE in the New Year's honours list for his services to charity. Some years later, in 1995, a further honour was bestowed on the promoter. His vast contribution to the sport of boxing was recognised when he was inducted into the International Boxing Hall of Fame.

Two Future World Heavyweight Champions

When watching the Henry Cooper and Cassius Clay contest, few, if any, of the spectators realised at the time that they were witnessing not one, but two future world heavyweight champions in action. Clay, of course, would go on to become the undisputed king when defeating Sonny Liston for the title on 25th February 1964. Liston retired in the sixth round of fifteen due to a shoulder injury. The battleground for the Clay-Liston contest had been the Convention Centre, Miami Beach, Florida, USA. On the Clay-Cooper undercard, Jimmy Ellis was also in action and won his bout, knocking out his opponent, Johnny Halafihi of Tonga, in the opening stanza in a contest scheduled for ten. Ellis went on to win the vacant WBA world heavyweight title, out-pointing Jerry Quarry over fifteen rounds at the Coliseum Arena, Oakland, California, on 27th April 1968.

First Time on the Canvas

Henry Cooper did remarkably well to find the punch to put Cassius Clay on the canvas during their encounter. Cooper was later stopped in round five of ten by the American, but his performance against Clay gave him hero status and enhanced his reputation worldwide.

The first man to have put Clay on the deck in the paid ranks was Sonny Banks on 10th February 1962 at Madison Square Garden, New York. Clay was down in the first stanza. He later stopped Banks in the fourth round of ten.

The third was Joe Frazier, who floored Clay – now named Muhammad Ali – in the fifteenth and final round, in defence of the undisputed world heavyweight title. The contest took place on 8th March 1971 at Madison Square Garden. On this occasion, Ali failed to regain the title, losing a fifteen-round points decision to Frazier. This was Ali's first defeat in the professional ranks.

The fourth to put Muhammad Ali, then the reigning undisputed world heavyweight champion, on the canvas was Chuck Wepner, on 24th March 1975, who achieved this feat in the ninth round when challenging for the crown. The venue for the Ali-Wepner contest was the Richfield Coliseum, Richfield, Ohio. Ali extracted revenge for the indignity of the knockdown by later stopping Wepner in the fifteenth and final round of the contest.

Cassius Clay Becomes World Heavyweight Champion

After his contest with Henry Cooper, Cassius Clay returned to the USA, and in his next bout, he challenged Sonny Liston for the world heavyweight championship. Many experts felt that Clay would be destroyed by Liston, who was a fearsome puncher and looked invincible. He was a wrecking ball. Liston was a one-man army who took no prisoners inside the square ring. He took the pre-fight insults from Clay very much to heart. He didn't find his comments amusing at all; in fact, he took great offence to them. He didn't like being ridiculed by the younger fighter. Liston wanted to crush Clay badly for the disrespect he had shown towards him leading up to the fight.

Before their meeting, Clay had taunted Henry Cooper, who took his barbs with a pinch of salt – it didn't trouble him at all, it was like water off a duck's back. Liston was not like the British fighter – he was a serious man and didn't find his comments even mildly funny. It appeared that Clay had pushed it a little too far this time with his antics. He'd bitten off more than he could chew with Liston and would painfully pay for doing so. Boxing cognoscenti feared the worst for the young challenger.

The title fight between Clay and Liston took place on 25th February 1964. It seemed a Liston win was a foregone conclusion. Everything pointed to that very fact. The fight between Clay and Liston would be very short, and the challenger would learn that if you play with fire, you will get burned.

However, at the Convention Center, Miami Beach, Florida, USA, Clay provided a shock when he dramatically dethroned Liston. The champion retired in the sixth round of fifteen. This was an amazing result for Clay, and one which turned the many doubters about his abilities into very firm believers. They knew from that moment on that he was a little special.

Cooper Adds European Title to His Name

After his defeat to Cassius Clay, Henry Cooper returned to the ring to put his British and Commonwealth heavyweight titles on the line against a rival he had shared the ring with on two previous occasions. The fighter in question was Brian London, from whom he had won the titles on 12th January 1959, with a fifteen-round points decision. There was also a bonus for the two combatants thrown into the mix – the vacant European championship would also be on the line.

The venue where Cooper and London were to exchange punches was Earl's Court Arena, Kensington, London. Since his defeat against Cooper, London had fought fourteen times, winning eight and losing six. This took his tally to forty fights, consisting of thirty victories, with ten defeats.

In his last venture into the ring, London had fought Bill Nielsen of the USA on 2nd December 1963, at the New St. James Hall, Newcastle, Tyne and Wear. The contest was scheduled for ten rounds. London did not need to travel the full distance; he made short work of the contest when he knocked out his opponent in the fourth stanza. Nielsen was not highly ranked, but it was still an impressive display by London.

Cooper's stock was now as high as it had ever been during his time in the sport, due to his contest against Cassius Clay. Cooper was a hero, the man of the moment. He may have lost to Clay, but he had acquitted himself well against the undefeated fighter from the USA, and had gained many more fans due to his valiant effort against the American. Much was now expected from Cooper in this defence against London.

Both champion and challenger left their corners on 24th

February 1964 at the Kings Hall, Belle Vue, Manchester, with a strong determination to be victorious. Cooper's timing was superb from the start – his left hand scored constantly. London attempted to get close to Cooper and work his body, but he was unable to make any impact or unsettle him in any way. There was always the fear that Cooper, who was prone to cuts, might sustain an injury that could see him suffer a defeat.

As always, the spectators were waiting for the champion to land the left hook, but he failed to do so. While London was able to avoid the punch that would end his challenge, he took a degree of punishment from the champion and refused to wilt. The fight went the full fifteen rounds, of which there was no doubt that Cooper had done more than enough to retain his British and Commonwealth titles with a points decision. By being victorious in six British title fights, Cooper had won his second Lonsdale belt outright and added the European crown to his name.

Old Adversary

The previous holder of the European title before Henry Cooper was Ingemar Johansson of Sweden – an old adversary of Cooper, who relinquished the crown upon retiring from the sport. In his first attempt to win this championship, Cooper was knocked out in round five of a scheduled fifteen on 19th May 1957. The battleground for the encounter was Johanneshov Ice Stadium, Stockholm.

London's Last Contest

After his failure to regain the British and Commonwealth heavyweight titles from Henry Cooper, London took part in a further seventeen fights, of which he won seven, lost nine and drew one. During his career, London challenged twice for the world heavyweight crown.

The first occasion took place on 1st May 1959, against Floyd Patterson at the Fairgrounds Coliseum, Indianapolis, Indiana, USA. London failed in his attempt when he was knocked out in round eleven of fifteen.

The second attempt came on 6th August 1966, against Muhammad Ali, for the WBC heavyweight title.

The champion easily knocked out London in the third stanza of fifteen. The venue for the contest was Earl's Court Arena, Kensington, London.

London participated in his last professional bout on 12th May 1970 at the Empire Pool, Wembley, London, against Joe Bugner. The contest saw Bugner stop London in the fifth round of a scheduled ten. It was clearly time for London to hang up the gloves, depart the sport, and seek new horizons outside of the ring.

During his professional career, Brian London had taken part in fifty-eight bouts, of which he won thirty-seven, lost twenty, and drew one.

The First Since Bruce Woodcock and Freddie Mills

The Henry Cooper-Brian London contest was the first time that two British fighters had fought each other with both the European, British and Commonwealth heavyweight titles at stake since 2nd June 1949. On that occasion, the defending title holder Bruce Woodcock was also putting the European, British and Commonwealth titles on the line against his challenger Freddie Mills, whose interest in the bout came to an end when he was knocked out in round fourteen of fifteen. The venue for the bout was the White City Stadium, White City, London.

Cooper Losses European Heavyweight Crown

On 28th September 1964, Henry Cooper lost the European heavyweight crown without even stepping into the ring. The title loss was due to the fact that he was unable to defend the championship by the stipulated date. He therefore had to relinquish the crown. This was a shame, since the championship was an important one to hold. The title had the potential to deliver to the holder lucrative fight dates and a shot at the world heavyweight crown.

Chapter Nine

Karl Mildenberger Wins European Heavyweight Title

Mildenberger Takes Over from Cooper

On 17th October 1964, Karl Mildenberger of Germany replaced Henry Cooper as the European heavyweight champion when he contested the vacant crown and thus became the new title holder. He won the championship with extreme ease when he knocked out Santo Amonti of Italy in the opening stanza of fifteen.

The venue for the Mildenberger-Amonti contest was the Deutschlandhalle, Charlottenburg, Berlin, Germany. Southpaw Mildenberger was a good fighter, but his claim to the crown was somewhat overshadowed by Cooper, who was still considered in many quarters to be the best heavyweight in Europe at that time. It was felt that Mildenberger would have to eventually meet Cooper to prove his right to the championship.

A Shock for Cooper

Roger Rischer arrived from the USA with a record of thirty-six bouts, consisting of twenty-six wins, eight defeats, with two draws. Rischer, at first sight, did not look to be too threatening.

In his last bout on 2nd November 1964, he had retained his California State Athletic Commission heavyweight title against Willie Ray Richardson by a stoppage in round eleven, in a scheduled twelve-round contest. That was not exactly an earth-shaker of a result, and the win meant very little when looking at the big picture in the heavyweight division.

The venue for the Rischer-Richardson bout had been the Civic Auditorium, San José, California. Truthfully, Rischer did not look like a world beater, and logically, it looked like a win for Cooper was very much on the cards.

On 16th November 1964 at the Royal Albert Hall, Kensington, London, Rischer sprang a nasty and unwanted surprise when he won a ten-round points decision over the British fighter. This wasn't supposed to happen. It was far from being an epic contest between the pair. Cooper failed to get going. He just wasn't able to stamp his authority on the contest. It just wasn't his night – a bad day at the office, or more to the point, a bad night in the ring. There was no way to hide the fact that this was a setback for the British fighter, one he could have done without.

Cooper had been riding the crest of a wave from his heroic bout with Cassius Clay. However, the defeat against Rischer brought Cooper down to Planet Earth with a bump. One day you're up, one day you're down. Boxing, like life, can be cruel. These kinds of setbacks often happen in the sport.

All Cooper could now do was draw a line under this fight. Rest and come back with the determination to get his name back in the win column. From his history in the ring, fans knew that Cooper was more than capable of doing so.

Defeats Wipperman

Dick Wipperman was the next fighter from the USA to share the ring with Henry Cooper. Cooper had to put his last losing contest against Roger Rischer behind him, turn back the visitor from the States, and hopefully put on an impressive show in doing so. Wipperman came with a record of thirty-one bouts, winning twenty-six, losing four, with one drawn. That wasn't a bad resumé. One which suggested that he was not going to be a walkover for Cooper.

In his last bout, which had taken place on 13th November 1964, Wipperman lost a ten-round points decision to the promising Oscar Bonavena of Argentina at Madison Square Garden, New York. There was no getting away from the fact that the contest against Wipperman was an important fight for Cooper. He had to win – a defeat was unthinkable, since a loss would certainly affect his world ranking even further.

However, Cooper was on form – he was able to get back on the winning trail. He showed his class on 12th January 1965, stopping his opponent in round five of a scheduled ten at the Royal Albert Hall, Kensington, London. Wipperman, as expected, did not come to roll over. He made a fight of it before the end came, giving the Briton a variation of problems to solve along the way.

A Regular Visitor to the UK

Chip Johnson from the USA was the next opponent to confront Henry Cooper on 20th April 1965 at the Civic

Hall, Wolverhampton, West Midlands. He came armed with a tally of sixteen bouts consisting of nine wins six defeats with one drawn.

Johnson was no stranger to UK boxing fans, he had fought in Britain on three previous occasions with a degree of success. His first bout in Britain had taken place on 29th September 1964, when he drew over ten rounds with Johnny Prescott at the Embassy Sportsdrome, Birmingham, West Midlands.

Then he stepped in with Jim Cooper (Henry's brother) and won by a stoppage in round three of eight on 9th November 1964, the venue for the contest being the Free Trade Hall, Manchester, Lancashire. (Jim Cooper retired from boxing soon after this bout.)

On 15th December 1964, he faced former British and Commonwealth heavyweight king Brian London at the Civic Hall, Wolverhampton, which saw his winning run come to an end. He was stopped in round four of ten by London, who was very much on form.

When Johnson left his dressing room to face Cooper, he was up against a determined fighter. He knew that Cooper would be a difficult man to defeat, but he felt that he was in with a chance of victory. No fighter enters the ring with a negative attitude, even when the odds are not in his favour. Johnson was no exception.

Once inside the ring, Cooper gazed at his opponent from his corner before the bell rang to start the contest. The British fighter was clearly taking stock of the man whom he was about to exchange leather with. Cooper moved swiftly from his corner to engage the man from across the pond. It appeared that the fight would go a few rounds before

Cooper would stop his man. That wasn't so – Cooper looked sharp, and made short work of Johnson, knocking him out in the first stanza of ten.

The American was dismissed with comparative ease by the British boxer. Cooper hardly worked up a sweat while the bout lasted. No doubt it was in Cooper's mind that this was the man who had beaten his brother. So the honour of the Cooper family was well and truly restored.

Henry exercising.

Henry taking a well-earned break.

Don Cockell, Joe Erskine, Henry, Len Harvey, Jack Peterson, Johnny Williams, Tommy Farr and Rocky Marciano.

Henry training with Danny Holland.

Henry training at the Thomas A Becket Gym.

Henry being interviewed at the Thomas A Becket Gym.

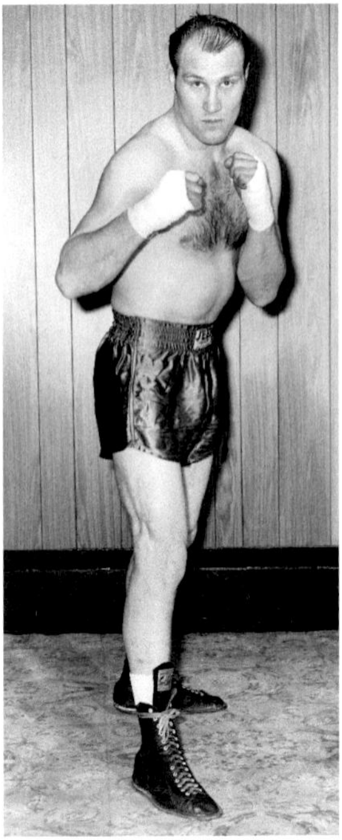

(above) Jack Bodell.
(above right) Henry and wife, Albina.
(middle right) Bombardier Billy Wells with Henry.
(bottom) Henry fights Muhammad Ali.

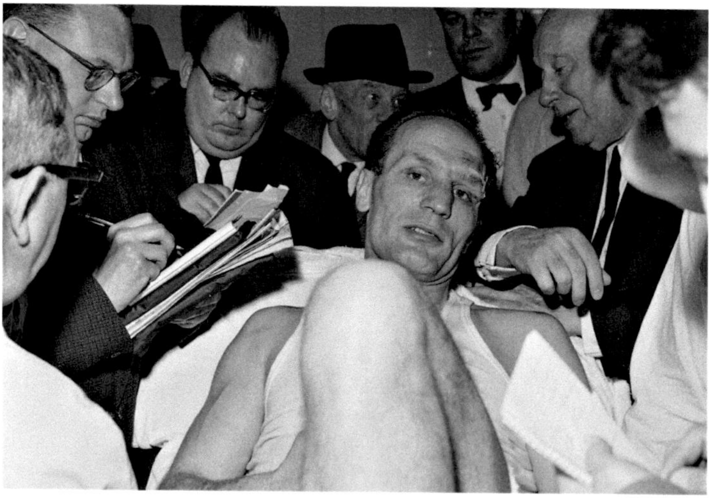

After Muhammad Ali fight.

Joe Bygraves Vs Ed Corlett.

BWC dinner. Joe Bugner and Henry.

BWC dinner. George Cooper, Billy Walker, Reg Gutteridge, Herbie Hide and Henry.

Henry.

BWC Dinner. Henry, Terry Spinks, Dick McTaggart and Billy Walker.

Frank Bruno, Horace Notice, Gary Mason and Harry Gibbs.

Ralph Oates and Henry.

Chapter Ten
Cooper Defeats Prescott

Prescott Fails in His Title Bid

Henry Cooper's next assignment was to defend his British and Commonwealth heavyweight titles against Johnny Prescott on 15th June 1965.

The venue for the Cooper-Prescott contest was St. Andrew's (Birmingham City FC), Birmingham, West Midlands. Prescott's record consisted of thirty-five fights, with twenty-six wins, six defeats, with three draws. Coming into the ring to confront Cooper, Prescott had lost his last two contests.

On 27th October 1964, he was disqualified in round eight of ten against Bill Nielsen of the USA. The venue for the bout was the Empire Pool, Wembley, London.

Then, on 22nd March 1965, he faced American Hubert Hilton at the Ice Rink, Nottingham, and once again lost when stopped in the fourth stanza of ten. It really wasn't going too well for Prescott at this stage of his career; to say things looked a little bleak was an understatement.

While one cannot always be certain when predicting the winner of a contest, it looked like a good bet to say that Cooper would retain his titles against his latest challenger, giving him his third successive defeat in a row. Prescott had the reputation of being a game fighter who always gave his best. He never left the ring without putting in every ounce of effort against his opponent, but sometimes that just wasn't enough. Sometimes you need a little more than that to see you through.

From the get-go, Cooper showed that he was a class above his challenger and was at no time at risk of being defeated. He outboxed Prescott, taking him to school, out-punching him throughout the fight. It was a painful night for the challenger, perhaps the most painful he had endured to date, while in the ring.

During the contest, Prescott was put on the canvas three times. Some fighters may well have chosen to stay on the canvas and get counted out, rather than continue to take the kind of blows Cooper was delivering, but not Prescott. That wasn't his style; while he was able to stay upright, he would fight. The challenger had clearly been hurt several times, but he bravely soaked up the punishment which came his way and fought on. Prescott pushed forward, ever hopeful of finding a way to defeat his tormentor. Prescott had to be admired for his courage, of which he had a great deal. He simply had no quit in him. His bravery was fully on display in this contest against Cooper. He stood and traded with the champion, even while he must have known deep down that he was in a losing battle, with no way back.

However, no matter how brave, no matter how tough, a man can only take so much punishment. The end finally came when Prescott retired in round ten of fifteen. There was no shame in the retirement. He had nothing left to give – the well had run dry. No one could fault Prescott's effort in the contest. He had given his all.

On gaining victory over Prescott, the champion put the first notch on a third Lonsdale belt. At this moment, Cooper was in a good place, career-wise.

Prescott and Cooper's Brother

Henry Cooper's brother Jim had also boxed Johnny Prescott in a bout that had taken place on 12th March 1963. Cooper won when he stopped Prescott in round two of ten, in a contest at the Embassy Sportsdrome, Birmingham, West Midlands.

Prescott's Last Contest

After his failure to win the British and Commonwealth heavyweight titles from Henry Cooper, Johnny Prescott participated in a further thirteen bouts, of which he won eight, lost four, with one draw.

He entered the ring for the last time on 20th January 1970, whereupon he lost via an eight-round points decision to Joe Bugner at the Royal Albert Hall, Kensington, London. Prescott had reached the end of the road, and the retirement decision he made was the correct thing to do.

During his professional career, Johnny Prescott took part in forty-nine contests, of which he won thirty-four, lost eleven, and drew four.

Johnson Derails Cooper

Henry Cooper entered the ring at the Empire Pool, Wembley, London, on 19th October 1965, to exchange punches with Amos Johnson of the USA.

Johnson arrived in the UK with a resumé of twenty-four bouts, winning nineteen, with three defeats, and two draws. The man from across the pond did not look too special – obviously he was a capable performer, but there was little to suggest that he would return to the states with a win under his belt.

In his last outing on 18th February 1965, he had knocked out Tex Tiger Gorman in round one of ten, the venue being the High School Gym, Medina, Ohio. The win was no big deal and proved very little. It was hardly one to spark any fear, or indeed panic, into the Cooper camp. Before that contest, Johnson had travelled to Germany to ply his trade on 20th November 1964, where he'd faced a much sterner test than he had against Gorman. The man in the opposite corner was Karl Mildenberger. To his credit, Johnson did well, holding the German to a ten-round draw. Johnson and Mildenberger fought at the Deutschlandhalle, Charlottenburgh, in Berlin.

A Cooper win was expected against Johnson, but the visiting American produced a shock by out-pointing the British fighter over the duration of ten rounds. Perhaps the Mildenberger result should have been a red flag and served notice that Johnson was no mug and wouldn't fold when put under pressure. The American showed this trait against Cooper. At that particular moment, it looked as if Cooper could say goodbye to any chance of getting a world title shot in the near future. It seemed that the ship had well and truly sailed, with the defeat against Johnson putting an end to any such aspirations. The losing contest against Johnson was one where Cooper really should have emerged victorious, one where an inside-the-distance win looked more than likely for him.

Once again, it was a reminder that in boxing, nothing is ever guaranteed. Three fights later, Johnson returned to the UK and met former British and Commonwealth Heavyweight King, Brian London, on 21st June 1966 at the Stadium, Liverpool, Merseyside. On this occasion, Johnson looked a little below par, which saw an on-form London take control of the contest from the start. The fight came to an end in round seven of a scheduled ten, when Johnson was disqualified for illegal use of his head.

First Man to Stop Hilton

Hubert Hilton of the USA was the next to go into the battle zone with Henry Cooper. He came with a resumé of seventeen fights, which consisted of thirteen victories, two defeats, and two draws. This was a must-win for Cooper after his last disappointing loss to Amos Johnson. The American had fought twice in the UK before and had been successful in said fights. Britain had proven to be a happy hunting ground for him.

His first outing was against Johnny Prescott on 22nd March 1965 at the Ice Rink, Nottingham. Prescott was stopped in the fourth session of ten by Hilton.

Following this victory, the American stepped in with Jack Bodell at the Hilton Hotel, Mayfair, London on 24th May 1965, and won by a stoppage in the sixth stanza of ten.

Before facing Cooper, Hilton had lost a ten-round points decision to Roberto Davila in Peru, at the Estadio Nacional, Lima. Davila was a competent campaigner who could be a handful for any fighter on his night. So this defeat did not devalue Hilton's worth in any way.

The American arrived back in Britain expecting to get

another win on his resumé. He must have felt that if Amos Johnson could beat Cooper, so could he. It may not be a case of it being easy-peasy, but he was confident that he had the skill set to sink Cooper and register another win in Britain. The home fighter was in no mood to accommodate Hilton in his quest for victory, and duly ended such expectations.

The bout between Cooper and Hilton took place at the Olympia, Kensington, London, on 25th January 1966. Cooper well and truly redeemed himself in this outing in some style, after the defeat in his last bout against Johnson. Cooper didn't waste any time getting down to work. He quickly stopped Hilton, courtesy of his left hook in round two of ten. In this victory, Cooper became the first man to stop Hilton in the paid ranks. This was a good showing by the British fighter – one he badly needed, and one which enhanced his world ranking to some degree.

Jefferson Out in One

Another boxer from the USA was the next to go into the ring with Henry Cooper. Jefferson Davis was his name.

The venue where the two met was the Civic Hall, Wolverhampton, West Midlands on 16th February 1966. Jefferson had competed in thirty-four bouts, winning twenty-six, losing seven, with one draw. He had fought in the UK before, on 22nd October 1963, at the Empire Pool, Wembley, London. In that contest, he came away with an unexpected win, stopping Jim Cooper (Henry's brother) in round seven of a scheduled eight.

In his last bout, before throwing leather against Cooper, Jefferson had a good win in Germany over Albert Westphal at the Deutschlandhalle, Charlottenburg, Berlin. On that outing, Davis won a ten-round points decision over the home fighter, showing both skill and resilience in doing so. Jefferson had been in the ring with some good names from whom he had learned a great deal about ring craft over the years. It seemed that while he was not favoured to get a victory over Cooper, there was the distinct possibility that he might give him a few testing moments during the contest, and there was, of course, the ever-present fear of Cooper sustaining a cut eye. That black cloud was always hanging over Cooper whenever he laced up a pair of gloves to fight, but nothing could have been further from the truth in this contest; the black cloud never came into sight.

Cooper was ready to rock and roll, and he had an early night after dispatching his opponent in the first round of a contest set for ten. This was the first time that Jefferson had been stopped inside the distance during his professional career. This looked good for Cooper and enhanced his reputation. He was flying high after his victories over both Jefferson Davis and Hubert Hilton.

Chapter Eleven

Cooper's World Title Challenge

Cooper's Big Moment

It was now the big moment for Henry Cooper – a challenge for the world heavyweight championship. For a boxer, it doesn't get any better – or indeed bigger – than this. The chance of a lifetime. The opportunity to be king of the world. The man who was putting the WBC heavyweight title on the line was Muhammad Ali, formerly Cassius Clay.

Cooper had famously decked Ali in their first encounter, landing with his left hook in round four of ten, on 18th June 1963. He came very close to becoming the first man to beat the undefeated fighter from the USA, until a cut eye in the fifth stanza ended Cooper's hope of victory.

The Cooper-Ali return was the fight that everyone in Britain was talking about. Newspapers and television were full of stories about the upcoming contest. Boxing was big news again, thanks to Cooper and Ali. It could be said that the nation was gripped with Ali-Cooper mania. The champion had to be respected for coming back to Britain to face the man who almost knocked him out. Cooper was the underdog going into the bout. When based on the facts presented, Ali had beaten better opponents than the British fighter had, and he'd improved greatly since their first fight.

Then there was the challenger's Achilles Heel: the cut eyes, which really couldn't be ignored when considering his overall chances against the champion. Yet many held on to the hope that Cooper's left hook, 'Enry's 'Ammer' would find Ali's chin once again, and this time put his lights out, thus seeing Cooper gain revenge for his previous defeat and bring the heavyweight title back to the UK. It's often said that it only takes one punch to win a fight and upset the odds. Could Cooper land that one punch and make it count?

On 21st May 1966, it was show time, and the two fighters stepped into the ring to renew their acquaintance at Arsenal Football Stadium, Highbury, London. There was a reported attendance of 46,000 who turned out to watch the fight. Ali was now undefeated in twenty-three bouts since turning professional.

The defence against Cooper was his fourth, since winning the title from Sonny Liston on 25th February 1964 at the Convention Center, Miami Beach, Florida, by way of a six-round retirement in a scheduled fifteen.

Ali made his first defence against Liston in a return contest which took place on 25th May 1965, at the Central Maine Civic Center, Lewiston, Maine. Ali emerged victorious when he knocked out Liston in the opening stanza of fifteen. It was easy work for the champ – far easier than many expected.

In his second defence, he squared up to former world

heavyweight king Floyd Patterson at the Convention Center, Las Vegas, Nevada, on 22nd November 1966. Ali retained the title when he stopped Patterson in round twelve of fifteen. Patterson showed courage, but he didn't present a danger to the reign of Ali.

In his third defence, Ali turned back the challenge of Canadian George Chuvalo, a tough fighter who pushed Ali all the way on 29th March 1966. Ali duly won by a fifteen-point decision. This was the first time Ali had travelled this distance for a title fight. The venue for the Ali-Chuvalo title defence was the Maple Leaf Gardens, Toronto, Ontario, Canada.

Prior to the Cooper-Ali bout getting underway, the national anthems of both countries were played. This added even more magic to the moment. Many boxing stars were in attendance, and introduced from the ring was former world heavyweight champion Rocky Marciano; Karl Mildenberger, the reigning European heavyweight title holder; Ingemar Johansson, former world and European heavyweight champion; Larry Gaines, the former Commonwealth heavyweight king; Georges Carpentier, former world light-heavyweight champion; Terry Downes, the former world and British middleweight champion; and Billy Walker, a British heavyweight contender.

Each introduction was greeted with loud applause from the fans, who were geared up for a good night's boxing. When the bell sounded to start the contest, the roars of encouragement for Cooper from the spectators were deafening. Excitement like this for a boxing contest in the UK had not been experienced for many years, if at all. This was something very special, an occasion that would not be forgotten by the fans.

Everyone in Britain was rooting for Cooper, keeping their fingers crossed that the night would end with a glorious victory for the home fighter. Cooper's face was etched in concentration as he marched forward towards a dancing Ali, who was shooting out the occasional left jab. The world champion, for good reason, was watchful of Cooper's left hook and moved gracefully around the ring, not presenting his opponent with a sitting target. He knew he could not be static against his challenger.

Ali was no fool; he knew Cooper was a dangerous man. He could really land with his famed left hook, which could bring a fight to a sudden end once it exploded on the jaw of an opponent. Ali's fast hands complemented his fast feet, as he moved around the ring with the grace of a middleweight. The challenger was the aggressor, looking to land his heavy artillery on the champion. The tension in the stadium was at an all-time high. Every man in attendance was willing Cooper on, in the hope that he would produce the payoff punch and change the shape of heavyweight boxing.

The fight was gripping in every sense of the word, as the two men exchanged jabs in the centre of the ring. Cooper continued to press and was always dangerous – looking for an opening to land his left hook, to separate Ali from his senses and also the title he held. Cooper was the embodiment of a man on a mission. Perhaps a 'mission impossible', considering he was up against a boxing master with outstanding speed, the kind of speed which had never been seen before from a heavyweight. Ali was evasive and hard to pin down. Cooper had to make Ali pay for any possible mistakes which he might make during the encounter.

Sadly, for Cooper, the champion didn't make many

mistakes, if any. Despite this, the Cooper was very much in the fight, on the front foot, constantly looking to find the punch which would make history. The punch which would see him become king of the division.

In the sixth round, the fear that many had held, transpired: Cooper's left eyebrow was cut, and it was bad. It was a horrific wound. The blood flowed freely down the challenger's face. It was apparent that his bid for the title was fast coming to an end. Cooper knew he just had seconds to land his famed left hook, but time wasn't on his side; it was fast running out. Ali knew once he saw the cut that the fight was his; he just had to keep his cool.

Cooper chased the champion, but Ali responded with fast jabs, jabs which further increased the damage to the cut. The blood continued to gush from Cooper's gaping wound, then onto his chest before finally landing on the canvas beneath his feet.

The referee finally stepped in and waved the fight over. His action in stopping the fight was no surprise. It was a massive disappointment for Cooper, and indeed the fans, who gave him every encouragement during the fight. No one could fault Cooper's performance – he gave it everything he had. Realistically, a Cooper victory and the likelihood of the fight going the full fifteen rounds was always a remote possibility, but Cooper's fans lived in hope. The whole of Britain lived in hope.

The British fighter lost, but he had been defeated by a fighter who would be recognised in the fullness of time as one of the greatest heavyweight world title holders, if not the greatest of them all, to enter the ring. In that, Cooper could take a degree of consolation.

Weights for the Contest

The reported weight of Henry Cooper during his challenge for the world heavyweight title was 13st 6lbs, while Muhammad Ali came into the ring at 14st 5 1/2lbs.

Heights of Both Boxers

Muhammad Ali stood at a reported height of 6ft 3inches, and Henry Cooper, 6ft 2inches during their contest for the world heavyweight crown.

Harry Levene

Harry Levene was the promoter of the Ali-Cooper WBC world heavyweight title bout. Thus, Levene can lay claim to promoting the most important fight of Cooper's career.

First Time Watching Her Husband

The world heavyweight title challenge by Henry Cooper against Muhammad Ali was the first time that Albina, Henry's wife, attended one of his bouts. Before this occasion, she would wait at home and watch his bout on television, or listen to it on the radio.

First Scot

George Smith was the third man in the ring with Henry Cooper and Muhammad Ali. He was an experienced official who handled the contest impeccably. In doing so, he became the first Scottish referee to be in charge of a world heavyweight title contest.

For the WBC World Heavyweight Title

The Muhammad Ali-Henry Cooper contest was for the

WBC world heavyweight title. At the time, the WBA Champion was Ernie Terrell of the USA. Terrell had won the vacant crown on 5th March 1965, when he out-pointed fellow countryman Eddie Machen over fifteen rounds at the International Amphitheatre, Chicago, Illinois. Ali had been stripped of the WBC version of the title when he went ahead, and made the first defence of the championship against Sonny Liston in a contest that took place on 25th May 1965 at the Central Maine Civic Center, Lewiston, Maine Central.

Ali emerged victorious when he knocked out Liston in the opening stanza of fifteen. While Terrell was a good fighter, his claim to the title was not taken too seriously by the purists of boxing. Ali was the champion and would remain so until he was beaten inside the ring for the title. At that time, it looked as if Ali was going to have a very long reign.

Muhammad Ali's Last Contest

After retaining the WBC world heavyweight title against Henry Cooper, Muhammad Ali boxed on a further thirty-seven occasions, winning thirty-two and losing five. Ali fought in his last professional contest on 11th December 1981, against Canada's reigning Commonwealth heavyweight title holder, Trevor Berbick. The contest took place at the Queen Elizabeth Sports Centre, Nassau in the Bahamas. Ali lost on points over ten rounds to Berbick, who would go on in the fullness of time to win the WBC world heavyweight championship. Everything in life comes to an end. Now, clearly, Ali's time in boxing had come to an end.

Muhammad Ali, who became the first man to win the

world heavyweight title on three separate occasions, took part in sixty-one professional contests, of which he won fifty-six, lost five, and had his name etched amongst the greats of boxing.

First Since Woodcock

The world heavyweight title fight between Muhammad Ali and Henry Cooper stirred up a frenzy that had not been seen before in the UK. It was a rare sight to see a world heavyweight championship staged in Britain. The last one had taken place on 6th June 1950, between Bruce Woodcock and Lee Savold from the USA, the venue being the White City Stadium, White City, London. The vacant world crown was on the line following the retirement of Joe Louis. The championship was only recognised by the British Boxing Board of Control.

In the USA, Ezzard Charles had taken the vacant version of the NBA heavyweight crown, out-pointing Jersey Joe Walcott over fifteen rounds at Comiskey Park, Chicago, Illinois, on 22nd June 1949. In truth, this version of the championship carried more credence than the Woodcock-Savold bout. There was a hope that Woodcock would defeat Savold and at least grab a piece of the title. A little bit of something is better than nothing at all. Woodock had previously met Savold at the Harringay Arena, Harringay, London, on 6th December 1948. On that occasion, Woodcock came out on top when Savold was disqualified in round four, in a contest set for ten. In the second meeting, Savold turned the tables when he took the victory and the title, after Woodcock retired in round four of fifteen, due to a badly cut eye.

The Eleventh Briton

Henry Cooper was the eleventh British boxer to have fought for the world heavyweight championship over the years.

The previous ten were:

Charlie Mitchell, who, on 25th January 1894, became the first Briton to challenge for the world heavyweight title. The reigning champion was James J. Corbett from the USA. The venue for the contest was the Duvall Athletic Club, Jacksonville, Florida. The end came when Corbett retained the crown by knocking out Mitchell in round three.

The championship came to the UK on 17th March 1897, when Bob Fitzsimmons knocked out the holder James J. Corbett in the fourteenth stanza. The bout took place at the Race Track Arena in Carson City, Nevada.

Bob Fitzsimmons lost the world heavyweight championship in his first defence on 9th June 1899, to James J. Jeffries of the USA, when knocked out in round eleven. The contest was staged at the Coney Island Athletic Club, Brooklyn, New York. He failed to regain the world heavyweight title when he met James J. Jeffries on 25th July 1902, when knocked out in the eighth stanza at the Arena, Athletic Club, San Francisco, California.

Gunner Moir stepped up to challenge for the global crown on 2nd December 1907. The reigning champion at the time was Tommy Burns of Canada. The fight took place at the National Sporting Club, Covent Garden, London. Burns retained the heavyweight title when he knocked out Moir in round ten. This was the first world heavyweight title bout to take place in the UK.

Jack Palmer climbed into the ring on 10th February 1908, at the Wonderland in Whitechapel Road, Whitechapel, London, to challenge for the world heavyweight title. The contest was all over in the fourth stanza, when defending title holder Tommy Burns knocked out Palmer to retain the crown.

Jem Roche failed in his attempt to win the world heavyweight crown when he was knocked out in the opening session by title holder Tommy Burns. The bout took place at the Theatre Royal, Dublin, Ireland, on 17th March 1908. Roche was born in Dublin, but at that time, Ireland was part of the UK.

Jewey Smith stepped between the ropes at the Neuilly Bowling Palace, Paris, France, to challenge Tommy Burns for the world heavyweight title on 18th April 1908. The title stayed with Burns when he knocked out Smith in round five.

Tommy Farr challenged world heavyweight champion Joe Louis of the USA for the title on 30th August 1937, at the Yankee Stadium, Bronx, New York. Farr failed to win the title when he lost a fifteen-round points decision. However, Farr became the first Briton to last the full distance in a world title contest.

Bruce Woodcock failed to win the vacant British and European version of the championship when he retired in the fourth round of fifteen against Lee Savold of the USA. The contest took place at the White City Stadium, White City, London, on 6th June 1950.

Don Cockell stepped up to challenge reigning world heavyweight champion Rocky Marciano of the USA on 16th May 1955, at the Kezar Stadium, San Francisco, California. Cockell's bid for the title ended when the referee stopped the contest in round nine of fifteen, in favour of Marciano.

Brian London entered the ring at the Fairgrounds Coliseum, Indianapolis, Indiana, to challenge Floyd Patterson of the USA on 1st May 1959. London failed in his bid when Patterson knocked him out in round eleven of fifteen.

Chapter Twelve

Patterson Defeats Cooper

Floyd Patterson

After the defeat to Ali, Cooper returned to the fray on 20th September 1966, at the Empire Pool, Wembley, London. It was not a gentle ease back into the ring for Cooper. His opponent was two-time world heavyweight champion Floyd Patterson from the USA. It could be said with some justification that Patterson's peak years were behind him, but he was still a formidable fighter, and he hadn't come to the UK to lose. The American was still ambitious.

Patterson was the first boxer in the history of boxing to regain the heavyweight crown, and the youngest at that time to have won it, at the age of twenty-one years, ten months, and twenty-six days. Like Cooper. Patterson had lost his last bout to Muhammad Ali, on 22nd November 1965, when bidding to regain the world heavyweight crown for the second time, at the Convention Center, Las Vegas, Nevada.

Ali proved too good for Patterson and stopped in round

twelve of fifteen. At the time of his fight with Cooper, Patterson had a resumé consisting of forty-eight fights, with forty-three victories and five defeats. There was a great deal riding on this contest for both men. The victor would have a great chance of securing another world title tilt down the line. Patterson had shared the ring during his fistic career with several outstanding fighters and had competed in twelve world title bouts, of which he won eight and lost four. That was some resumé to be proud of. Discounting Zora Folley, Ingemar Johansson and Ali, Patterson was one of the best fighters Cooper had boxed at that particular time.

It looked to be an intriguing contest between the two combatants, and it proved to be so. When the pair left their corners, the man from the USA looked very confident and moved around Cooper, looking for an opening to land his fast combinations. Patterson, with his peek-a-boo style, looked every inch a class act.

In the first two rounds, the two fighters looked well-matched, with neither man dominating the exchanges.

Then, in the third stanza, the situation changed. Patterson scored with his left hook, which sent Cooper down for a count. On getting back to his feet, Cooper looked stunned, but he resumed the battle until the bell sounded to end the round.

From that point on, the spectators began to sense that this contest might not go Cooper's way.

In the fourth round, Cooper attempted to land his left hook, but the American recognised the danger and cleverly blocked the punch. Patterson was no mug in the ring – he had seen it all in his time. His defence was excellent; he clearly knew his craft. Try as he might, Cooper was unable to land anything with significant force to deter his opponent. Patterson's hand speed was exceptional.

Once again, Cooper touched down on the canvas from a blow he received from the American. Patterson was really warming to the task, boxing superbly. A Cooper defeat now seemed more than imminent, with each passing moment. Cooper had to pull something out of his bag of tricks to take the advantage away from his opponent, or execute his own left hook to finish Patterson off, if he was to avoid defeat. That was, of course, easier said than done. Cooper was unable to up his work rate against his foe. Patterson always appeared to be one step ahead of him.

The American finally put Cooper's lights out when he caught him once more in the round with a right hook, which knocked him out. The British fighter crashed down face-first after taking the blow.

The bout was scheduled for ten rounds, but it would have been optimistic to believe that the fight would go the full distance. This was a downer for both Cooper and the home fans, who really hoped that a victory would seal a magnificent night for British boxing and hence see Cooper back in the running for another world title shot. How the UK fans would have loved to have seen a third meeting between Ali and Cooper. That would have been a booster for British boxing; a bout guaranteed to pull in the punters once more.

Cooper and Patterson showed great sportsmanship and respect towards each other before and after the bout. They were a credit to the sport. The loss was a disappointment for Cooper, but he still had his British and Commonwealth titles to fall back on, so it was not all doom and gloom for him. His future still looked good on the domestic front, and even the European title would be within his sights. For Patterson, he could now look forward to challenging once again for the world crown.

Ellis Beats Patterson

In his fifth bout after beating Henry Cooper, Floyd Patterson fought the then reigning WBA world heavyweight title holder Jimmy Ellis, on 14th September 1968. The contest took place at the Rasunda Fotbollsstdion, Stockholm, Sweden. Patterson was hoping that he would once again hold a version of the world championship for a third time, but he failed to lift the title when he lost a fifteen-round points decision.

Cooper Beats Jacobs

Boston Jacobs, another boxer from the USA, was the next to go against Cooper on 17th April 1967. The fighter from across the pond was no Muhammad Ali, nor a Floyd Patterson – he was nowhere near their class. He was short on experience, joining Cooper in the ring with a resumé of ten bouts, consisting of seven wins and three defeats.

In his last visit to the ring, Jacobs met opponent Willie Ray Richardson, whom he stopped in the fourth stanza of ten. The contest took place on 2nd February 1967. The venue for Jacobs-Richardson bout had been the Exposition Building, Portland, Maine. Cooper could not be complacent against Jacobs; he was coming to battle with two successive defeats behind him. The last thing Cooper needed was another loss on his record. He needed to get his name back in the win column.

A defeat for Cooper would've been a total disaster, especially against a man with so few fights on his slate. The question was, did Cooper still have the ambition and the fire in his soul to gain a victory, even against a man who really had moderate skills, when compared to his own?

When looking at the form line of the two fighters, a Cooper win was expected inside the scheduled distance, but that failed to happen. Cooper won well enough at the De Montfort Hall, Leicester, in Leicestershire, but it was by a ten-round points decision. Cooper was always in charge of the contest, but it was a little disappointing that he was unable to lower the axe on Jacobs and halt him before the final session.

However, the important thing is, when looking at the big picture, Cooper got the win, and that's what counts in the final analysis.

Bodell Challenge

Henry Cooper was back in the ring on 13th June 1967 to defend his British and Commonwealth titles. His challenger was Jack Bodell, who came to battle with a resumé of forty-nine fights, consisting of forty-one wins and eight defeats. The challenger had won his last six bouts in a row, his last defeat having taken place on 28th June 1966, against Italian Piero Tomasoni, being stopped in the third round of ten at the Royal Albert Hall, Kensington, London. Bodell always came into the ring to fight, and he would give everything he had to gain a victory over Cooper. The man could not be sold short.

When the bell rang to start the fight, Bodell came out of the starting blocks like a greyhound after the hare, attacking Cooper with his right jab, which found its way through his defence. One could see by his body language that the challenger really fancied the job. He seemed to be throwing caution to the wind – walking into Cooper, throwing an array of punches. The title holder was clearly taken out of his stride by his opponent's fast start. Bodell must have felt that this was his time to take over as champion. Cooper looked sluggish and was having difficulties with the southpaw stance of Bodell. The challenger came forward relentlessly. The champion countered, but his timing seemed to be a little off. There was no argument that Cooper was having a hard time against his challenger, who had taken him completely by surprise.

When round two started, Bodell looked to continue where he left off, unloading on the champion, throwing punch after punch. He was setting a hectic pace – one which Cooper seemed to have trouble keeping up with. The challenger was looking good, forcing Cooper backwards. The champion was already looking a little shop-worn and weary. Cooper needed to come up with something soon, if he was to hold on to his titles. The fight really wasn't going his way. Cooper needed to move up a gear and take control, and gain Bodell's respect by scoring with some hurtful punches to stop his advance.

Then, if Cooper didn't already have enough problems to contend with, he sustained a cut between his eyes. It had to be wondered if this was the beginning of the end for Cooper's championship reign, and there was to be a changing of the guard in the heavyweight division. The challenger was making it a war of attrition – he was enjoying every moment of the battle. The bloodied face of Cooper buoyed Bodell; he grew more confident with each passing second. He must have felt that he was only minutes away from becoming the new champion.

Then, Cooper dashed all of Bodell's aspirations of becoming the newly-crowned title holder in an instant. He saw his opening and struck, unleashing his left hook, which found its way through Bodell's defences, exploding onto his jaw. The punch instantly had Bodell in trouble, leaving him floundering across the ring. He had no control of his legs, which had turned to jelly. Bodell was now desperately attempting to survive, let alone win. His bid for the titles was all but over. The champion knew he had his man heading for the door marked 'way out' and went for the finish. It was a well-established fact that Cooper knew how to finish his man once he had him on the hook. Cooper let his hands go and punished Bodell. The challenger was left helpless on the ropes when the referee called an end to the bout. Cooper had a few rocky moments at the Molineux Grounds, Wolverhampton, West Midlands, during the title bout, but he came through like a true champion and retained his titles. He could now look forward to more rewarding bouts in the future.

Cooper Relinquishes Championship

During 1968, Henry Cooper relinquished his long-held British heavyweight championship, sending the title back to the British Boxing Board of Control. This action was taken by Cooper as the Board refused to sanction his proposed world title shot at the reigning WBA 137 heavyweight champion Jimmy Ellis. The British board were not, at that time, a member of that organisation. Cooper, however, held on to his Commonwealth title.

Jack Bodell Wins British Heavyweight Title

After being stopped on his feet by Henry Cooper in his bid for the British and Commonwealth heavyweight championship, Jack Bodell didn't give up on his dream of winning the British crown. He continued with his career, winning his next eleven bouts on the bounce. Then, on 13th October 1969, he had another shot at the British heavyweight title. This opportunity came about when Cooper relinquished the title. Bodell was then matched with Welshman Carl Gizzi for the vacant crown at the Ice Rink, Nottingham, Nottinghamshire. Bodell had previously defeated Gizzi on 27th November 1968, in a final eliminator for the British crown, stopping him in round two of a scheduled twelve at the Sophia Gardens Pavilion, Cardiff, Wales, by way of a cut-eye decision. The return contest with Gizzi went the full fifteen rounds. Bodell boxed well against the Welshman and was declared the new champion with a solid points decision.

Bodell the First

On winning the vacant British heavyweight title by defeating Carl Gizzi, Jack Bodell carved out his own piece of boxing history in the UK. He became the first boxer with the southpaw stance to hold the British crown in the division, a feat for which he will always be remembered.

Chapter Thirteen

Cooper Wins Third Lonsdale Belt Outright

Cooper Meets the Blond Bomber

After dispatching Jack Bodell with relative ease, Henry Cooper was next out on 7th November 1967 to meet Billy Walker, nicknamed the Blond Bomber. This was the fight everyone wanted to see – the big shootout. The meeting had been brewing for some time between the two fighters. Walker was well respected by fans of the sport. He fought with the heart of a lion; he always gave his all in every contest he took part in – be it a winner or a loser.

He was also a big puncher, which added to the appeal of their meeting. This was a promoter's dream. There were few empty seats, if any, whenever Walker boxed on the card. He always gave value for money. Cooper vs. Walker was a contest between two fighters who were both loved in equal measure by the fans. It was a natural pairing, an ideal match between two London boys, slugging it out in the ring for the championship of Britain and the Commonwealth.

The contest was talked about for weeks before it happened. The fight had really caught the imagination of the public in a big way. Walker entered the ring at the Empire Pool, Wembley, London, with loud cheers from the fans. This was a venue both he and Cooper knew well. Walker had previously boxed there on twelve occasions, and Cooper ten times. Walker came to battle with a resumé of twenty-eight bouts, winning twenty, losing six, with two draws. In his previous bout, Walker had challenged Germany's Karl Mildenberger on 21st March 1967, for the European heavyweight crown at the same venue where he was now to fight Cooper. Walker, as per usual, had given his best against Mildenberger, giving the crowds some exciting moments while the contest endured. The man was rarely in a dull fight, if at all.

The bout with Mildenberger came to a finish in round eight of fifteen, when the British challenger was stopped by the champion. The referee, in his wisdom, considered that Cooper had taken enough punishment. To his credit, Walker went out on his shield; the man was a warrior through and through. He would fight until the bitter end. Had Walker defeated Mildenberger, it would have added extra value to the contest, with him being a European champion.

Entering the bout, Cooper was the firm favourite, but Walker felt he had the style to oust the champion from the titles. Once the bell rang out to start proceedings, the fighters came quickly out of their corners and wasted no time in getting down to the business at hand. There would be no pussyfooting around. The round saw some lively exchanges between the two combatants. There was no feeling-out process between the two men. Both fighters felt they knew all they had to know about each other.

Walker, as always, stormed forward, attempting to pin Cooper down and trap him on the ropes, where he would be able to line him up for a series of damaging blows. Walker was fully in the zone, looking to land the payoff punch. However, the champion was having none of it – he was able to stay disciplined and box his way out of any potential danger. Cooper planted his feet and landed an array of stinging punches to his challenger's head. This did not discourage Walker in any way whatsoever. He continued to march forward after the champion. Cooper continued to land several quality shots during the round, with no apparent effect on the man standing in front of him. Walker stood his ground; he was as tough as they come, and just kept on going after Cooper, throwing leather. No one could accuse the challenger of having a glass jaw. Walker could take a punch, that was for sure. It was an interesting first stanza between the two fighters.

The second session looked ominous for Cooper, especially when he was cut over his left eye. This was not great news for him. The champion didn't panic as the blood ran down his face. He had been down this road many times before. Cooper knew how to handle what would be, for many fighters, a tricky moment. The sight of Cooper's cut must have given Walker the sense that he was close to pulling off a stoppage win, and was hence about to obtain the best victory of his career. While the challenger looked very strong at this stage, he was not able to capitalise on his success.

The champion called on his vast experience, and he was

able to keep his challenger at bay, scoring with his educated left jab. The action continued in the rounds which followed. There was no let-up, much to the delight of the loudly cheering fans. The two fighters were getting stuck in, both landing with the kind of punches that were potentially knockout blows.

The fifth session saw Walker sustain a cut over his right eye. So now it was even-steven, with both men now suffering with cuts. A stream of blood ran freely down Walker's face. Make no mistake: the two fighters trading blows had both contributed to the blood which had stained the canvas on which they were standing. Walker shook his head in frustration over the injury, but he kept going after the champion. There was no way the challenger was likely to last the full course with such a wound. It would now be an obvious target for Cooper to concentrate on with his sharp left jab and peck away at the injury, the intention being to open up the wound even further.

In the sixth stanza, it was all over when the referee stepped in to stop the bout, after carefully examining the damage to the challenger's cut. Walker was disappointed about losing in such a way. On entering the ring earlier, he felt it was his moment to take his place at the top of the domestic division. Cooper could identify with the situation, having lost due to his own history of cut eyes during his career.

The bout was set for fifteen rounds, but as always in a contest of this magnitude, no one truly felt the fight would go that distance. So the early closure to the contest came as no great surprise. It was an exciting bout while it lasted, and the fans certainly got good value for their hard-earned cash. This was a great night for Cooper, who had seen off a dangerous challenger. He was now on the lookout for other boxing opportunities.

Walker's Farewell

After being defeated by Henry Cooper in his bid for the British and Commonwealth heavyweight titles, Billy Walker resumed his career. He took part in two more contests, winning one and losing one. Walker had his final fight on 25th March 1969, when he was stopped in round eight in a scheduled twelve-round contest by Jack Bodell at the Empire Pool, Wembley, London. Walker, whose appearance in the ring always guaranteed excitement, knew that it was time to say goodnight and goodbye to the sport.

During his professional career, Billy Walker had taken part in thirty-one contests, of which he won twenty-one, lost eight, and drew two.

Three Lonsdale Belts

In his successful defence of the British and Commonwealth titles against Billy Walker, Henry Cooper added a new page to the history books of British boxing. He became the first boxer to win three Lonsdale Belts outright. To achieve this, Cooper had to win nine British championship fights.

Rule Change

The rules on winning a Lonsdale belt have since been changed; a boxer can only win one belt outright in any one weight division. A fighter will now have to score four British title victories to win a belt outright, rather than three. So the Henry Cooper record will not be equalled or surpassed in the future. So Cooper could quote with confidence the title of the George Gershwin song, 'They Can't Take That Away from Me.'

Introduction of the Belt

The National Sporting Clubs Challenge Belt was a much-desired trophy, won by boxers who had captured the British crown. The history of the belt dates back to 1909. The belt had been presented to the club by the 5th Earl of Lonsdale. Boxers who won the British title at the National Sporting Club would be rewarded with the belt. The prospect of winning the belt was an excellent inducement for any boxer who participated in the sport. This enabled the National Sport Club to keep control of British title bouts.

The first heavyweight to win the belt was Bombardier Billy Wells on 24th April 1911. Wells secured the belt when he knocked out opponent William 'Iron' Hague in the sixth stanza of twenty. The venue was the National Sporting Club, Covent Garden, London. The National Sport Club eventually came to an end in 1935. The British Boxing Board of Control then took over in 1936 and continued the practice of awarding the belt, which was now known as the Lonsdale Belt, to the fighters who won the domestic title.

Long-Serving Champion

At the time of defeating Billy Walker, Henry Cooper had held the British and Commonwealth heavyweight titles for a period of eight years, nine months and twenty-six days. That was an astonishing time to remain a champion. Cooper had hence set a record for holding the titles longer than any previous champion in the division. Cooper's name was truly synonymous with the British heavyweight title.

Karl Mildenberger

Henry Cooper was next given the chance to regain the European heavyweight crown against the serving holder, Karl Mildenberger of Germany. The contest took place on 18th September 1968, at the Empire Pool, Wembley, London. Mildenberger was making his seventh defence of the title against the Londoner. There was no denying that he had been a good champion during his reign. Mildenberger had captured the vacant crown on 17th October 1964, when he knocked out Italian Santo Amonti in the first stanza of fifteen at the Deutschlandhalle, Charlottenburg, Berlin, Germany. (The title had been vacated by Henry Cooper.)

In his previous contest before meeting Cooper, Mildenberger had been knocked out in round seven of a scheduled twelve-round contest by Leotis Martin of the USA. This bout took place at the Festhalle, Frankfurt, Hessen, Germany on 5th April 1968. Martin was a tough nut and a world-ranked fighter who was a nightmare for anyone to face inside the ring. So this defeat did not reflect too badly on the German's reputation or his capabilities. I think it would be a fair comment to say that Cooper would have had his hands full with Martin, had they met. Mildenberger entered the fray against Cooper with a resumé of sixty-one bouts, winning fifty-three, losing five, with three drawn.

On his way to the ring, Cooper was given a tremendous reception from the fans in attendance – the expectations for a win for the home fighter were high. In their minds, they could not for one minute foresee their man leaving the ring without the title belt strapped around his waist. Cooper looked on form from the opening bell. He was sharp and accurate with his punching. He moved well, taking the fight to the champion. It was encouraging to see that the southpaw stance of Mildenberger did not trouble Cooper in any way whatsoever. He was in charge of the fight from the start and looked on his way to certain victory. That victory came in the eighth round.

The fight concluded when the champion was disqualified. Cooper had been badly cut, and it was obvious to everyone that he could not continue to box with such a wound. The cut had been caused by a head-butt, an action that the referee had cautioned Mildenberger for a few times during the course of the bout. So once again, Cooper was the champion of Europe. It was a good night for Cooper. Cooper could now look forward to lucrative defences of the title in the future.

Mildenberger's Last Contest

The loss of the European heavyweight title to Henry Cooper proved to be the last time that Karl Mildenberger would slip on the gloves and venture into the ring to do battle. Soon after the defeat to Cooper, he retired from the sport. Mildenberger's name will be forever etched into the history books of boxing, as he became the first boxer with the southpaw stance to challenge for the world heavyweight championship. This event took place on 10th September 1966, when Mildenberger stepped into the ring to challenge Muhammad Ali for the WBC title. The venue for the Clay-Mildenberger contest was Waldstadion/Radrennbahn, Frankfurt, Hessen, Germany. Mildenberger gave it a worthy try, but failed in his bid when he was stopped in round twelve of fifteen.

During his professional career, Karl Mildenberger served boxing well, giving Germany a number of nights to remember. Many considered him to be the best German heavyweight boxer since Max Schmeling, who reigned as world champion from 12th June 1930 to 21st June 1933. Mildenberger took part in sixty-two professional bouts, of which he won fifty-three, lost six, and drew three.

Piero Tomasoni

Henry Cooper made the first defence of the European title (in his second reign) on 13th March 1969. His challenger was Italian Piero Tomasoni. The defence against Tomasoni took place at the Pala Eur, Roma, Lazio, Italy. The challenger had a resumé of forty-four bouts, consisting of thirty-three victories, six defeats, with five draws. While Cooper was considered to be a class above the Italian in ability and punching power, his opponent could not be dismissed lightly. Tomasoni was fighting on his own turf, in front of his own fans, who would cheer his every move, every punch which landed and even every punch which missed. This was his third attempt to win the championship.

The Italian's first crack at the title came on 14th May 1965, against the then-reigning title holder Karl Mildenberger, at the Festhalle, Frankfurt, Hessen, Germany. Mildenberger retained the championship with a fifteen-round points decision. The second attempt to add the title to his name came on 1st February 1967. Mildenberger was still the title holder, and Tomasoni returned to Germany to make his bid at the same venue, the Festhalle.

Once again, the Italian failed to win the title when he was outpointed over fifteen rounds. Going into the ring against Cooper, Tomasoni had every intention of making it a case of 'third time's the charm'. Perhaps he may have thought that Cooper might be on the slide and was ready for the taking. After all, Cooper had been boxing for a long time, and it was possible he was not the fighter he once was.

In his last bout before entering the ring to face Cooper, Tomasoni had defeated German Jurgen Blin on 29th September 1968, by a disqualification in round two of ten, in a contest which took place at Brescia, Lombardia, Italy.

On the night, the partisan fans were fully charged up and very much on the side of the home fighter. They wanted no less than to see their man bring the title back to Italy. It was apparent from the atmosphere at the venue that many of Tomasoni's supporters would be far from happy to see him defeated. The country's last champion at the weight was Franco Cavicchi, who reigned from 1955-1956.

However, Cooper was not without support – a number of fans had flown from Britain to Italy to give him their encouragement. The contest was also televised live in the UK, so many could watch the action from the comfort of their own homes. The fight was set for fifteen rounds, but once again, it was obvious that it would not go the full distance. The contest was short, but it had more than its share of drama and tension while it lasted.

During the contest, Cooper was floored twice by punches which were, shall we say, a little low to say the least. The champion was being given some rough treatment, the kind of treatment which was well outside of the rules of boxing. It really didn't look too good for the British fighter at this stage.

However, Cooper, angered by the treatment he was

receiving, clearly decided that enough was enough, and he would put an end to it once and for all. He took positive action and knocked Tomasoni out in the fifth round to retain the championship. The end was sudden, and as such, stunned the partisan fans into silence for a brief moment. They were not exactly overcome with joy, seeing their man defeated, and that's putting it mildly. Tomasoni felt the full force of the left hook and fell to the canvas, where he was counted out by the referee. Cooper returned from Italy to the UK shores with the title, and Tomasoni was left with a painful defeat and the knowledge that he would never hold the European heavyweight championship. It was a title beyond his reach. He had three bites of the apple. There wouldn't be a fourth.

Last Roll of the Dice

After his failed attempt to take the European title away from Henry Cooper, Piero Tomasoni fought on. He participated in two more bouts – and he lost both. It was clear from his performances that he was now on the decline.

On 1st December 1969, he attempted to regain the Italian Heavyweight title against holder Dante Cane. It was his last roll of the dice. A defeat would see him with no place to go. The Tomasoni-Cane contest took place in Bologna, Emilia-Romagna, Italy. Cane emerged victorious when he stopped Tomasoni in round eight of twelve.

After this result, the curtain came down on Tomasoni's career. He had entered the ring for the final time and had thrown his last punch. While he may not have been ranked alongside the best in the world, he was a decent heavyweight at the European level. Indeed, had Henry Cooper and Karl

Mildenberger not been around, there is every chance that he might well have won the European title. During his career, Piero Tomasoni took part in forty-seven bouts, of which he won thirty-three, lost nine and drew five.

An Unexpected Setback

After his successful defence of the European heavyweight title against Piero Tomasoni, Henry Cooper looked set to make further defences of the championship. Just when it seemed everything was going well, Cooper suffered a medical setback. Cooper was forced to relinquish his crown when he was forced to have a cartilage operation. The European heavyweight title vacated by Henry Cooper was eventually won by Peter Weiland of Germany, who knocked out Bernard Thebault of France in the first round of fifteen. The contest took place on 6th December 1969, at Osteehalle, Kiel, Schleswig-Holstein, Germany. When looking at the resumés of both Weiland and Thebault, I don't think it is too ungracious to say that had Cooper faced either one of them, he would have won without raising a sweat.

Chapter Fourteen

Defeats Bodell to Regain British Heavyweight Title

This is Your Life

Henry Cooper was surprised when he was the subject of the TV show *This is Your Life*, hosted by Eamonn Andrews. The show looked back at Cooper's life, with many faces from his past. Guests included Cooper's wife, Albina, his two brothers, Bernard and George (who boxed under the name of Jim), also his father, Henry Cooper Snr (his mother, Lilly, was unable to appear on the show due to having the flu). A film clip of Cooper's sons Henry Marco and John Pietro talking about their father was also shown. Bob Hill, who spotted the potential of Cooper when watching him sparring with friends, was also interviewed.

Boxers Billy Waker, Jack Bodell, Dick Richardson, and manager Jim Wicks also came onto the set and spoke in high praise about Cooper. Archie McAteer also appeared on the show – he was a youngster who recalled how he had once written to Cooper to ask how to perfect a left hook. To his pleasant surprise, Cooper responded to the request and was very helpful to him.

Then came the ultimate praise from the then former world heavyweight champion, Muhammad Ali, who tendered his good wishes for the British fighter in a transmission from the USA. He recalled in detail how Cooper had put him on the deck in their first encounter. It was a punch which had left an indelible impression on Ali.

The OBE

The OBE was presented to Henry Cooper in the 1969 New Year's Honours awards for his services to boxing. This was a well-deserved award for Cooper, who was more than pleased to be recognised in such a way. It also shone a bright light on the sport, of which Cooper was a fine representative, in and out of the square ring.

A Question of Sport

Henry Cooper and Cliff Morgan were the first team captains to appear on the very popular *A Question of Sport*, which was screened by the BBC on 5th January 1970. The quiz show was hosted by David Vine, and was an immediate hit with viewers.

Cooper and Brut

During the 1970s, Henry Cooper appeared in a series of TV advertisements for the 'Brut' aftershave and deodorant brand, which proved to be extremely popular. Cooper was often joined by other sportsmen like Barry Sheene (motorcycle racer) Kevin Keegan (footballer) and David Hemery (track and field athlete). Cooper would often say "Splash it all over!" during the commercials.

Cooper Regains British Heavyweight Title

Henry Cooper returned to the ring on 24th March 1970 to challenge Jack Bodell for the British heavyweight crown, and also to defend his Commonwealth title. The fans were pleased to see Cooper step back between the ropes after undergoing an operation on his knee. His popularity was as high as ever with the public. It was pleasing to see Cooper gloved up and ready for action. His absence from the ring left a void in the domestic division – a void which was difficult to fill. Cooper had been missed; there was no argument about that. The British public loved Cooper; he was their hero. Win or lose, he was their man.

The venue for the Cooper-Bodell contest was the Empire Pool, Wembley, London. Bodell had entered the ring on twelve occasions since his last confrontation with Cooper. He had fought and beaten the likes of Johnny Prescott, Brian London, and Billy Walker to earn his well-deserved second shot at the British heavyweight title. He had won the vacant championship when out-pointing Welshman Carl Gizzi over fifteen rounds on 13th October 1969, at the Ice Rink, Nottingham, Nottinghamshire. Bodell's resumé now read sixty-two bouts, with fifty-three wins and nine defeats. Bodell was more than confident that he would defeat Cooper, retain the British title, and add the Commonwealth crown to his name.

Should he succeed, he would then be in a position to go hunting for the European crown. There was no doubt that this version of Bodell was much better than the one who faced Cooper the first time around. He was both wiser and more experienced. He obviously felt that he had learned a great deal from his first meeting with Cooper, and he now had the necessary ring smarts to claim a victory.

Even so, Cooper was favoured to repeat the win over Bodell. Despite this, there was the ever-present concern about the possibility of cuts, which could curtail Cooper's route to victory. It had been one year and eleven days since Cooper last fought, due to his cartilage operation, so ring rust had to be a concern in this contest.

When the bell signalled to start the fight, the two men quickly left their respective corners and exchanged exploratory jabs. Cooper looked positive and moved around the ring with his hands in a protective position, ever alert to the danger Bodell might represent. Bodell was fired up and ready to go. He pumped his right jab into Cooper's face. He was keen to get stuck in and force the action. Cooper also scored with his left jab. The pair wasted little time getting to grips with each other. There was a great deal at stake for both Bodell and Cooper in this championship bout.

The spectators in attendance gave Cooper every encouragement with chants of, 'Henry! Henry!' echoing around the venue. There was no doubt who the fans favoured in this clash.

In the rounds which followed, Bodell made a valiant attempt to retain the British title and take the Commonwealth crown, but it was not enough. Cooper had an answer for everything Bodell tried in the contest. The British title holder was outmanoeuvred and outboxed by his opponent. Bodell, to his credit, was gutsy and did not give up. He fought on, in the hope that he might find a way to win. At the end of the fifteen-round encounter, it was no shock when Cooper's hand was raised in victory. He was once again the British champion. During the course of the contest, Bodell hit the canvas on two separate occasions, but rose to his feet and battled on until the end. He gave it his best shot, but it wasn't enough. Cooper looked as good as ever in this bout. It was evident that he still had a great deal left to give to boxing.

Eddie Thomas

Welshman Eddie Thomas was the 'cuts man' in Henry Cooper's corner during the Jack Bodell title bout. He had replaced Danny Holland, who had parted company with Jim Wicks. Thomas was a well-renowned boxing manager and trainer, who had taken a number of his charges to various titles. Thomas was well-versed with the sport, having had his own successful boxing career, winning the British, European and Commonwealth welterweight titles during his time in the ring. He had compiled a resumé which consisted of forty-eight bouts, winning forty, losing six, and drawing two.

First Notch

By regaining the British heavyweight title from Jack Bodell, Henry Cooper had now achieved ten victories, which involved the domestic title. Cooper had hence put the first notch on a potential fourth Lonsdale Belt. This was the first time that any boxer in the division had accomplished this feat.

First Since Len Harvey

In defeating Jack Bodell, Henry Cooper became the first man to regain the British heavyweight title since Len Harvey. On 30th November 1933, Harvey ventured into the ring and won the championship after out-pointing holder, Jack Petersen from Wales, over the duration of fifteen rounds.

The contest took place at the Royal Albert Hall, Kensington, London. Harvey lost the crown to Petersen in a return contest, which was staged at the White City Stadium, White City, London, on 4th June 1934, when stopped in round twelve of a scheduled fifteen.

Harvey also lost the Commonwealth title to Petersen, which he had previously won when defeating holder Larry Gains of Canada with a fifteen-round points decision on 8th February 1934. The venue for the Harvey-Gains bout was the Royal Albert Hall, Kensington, London. Harvey regained the British title on 1st December 1938, when he contested the then vacant crown against Eddie Phillips at the Harringay Arena, Harringay, London, by way of a disqualification in round four of fifteen. The British title had been vacated by Welshman Tommy Farr before this contest.

Won an Award twice

In 1970, Henry Cooper won the *BBC Sports Personality of the Year* award. On this occasion, Cooper had the distinction of becoming the first sportsman to win this prize twice. He had previously won the award in 1967.

Bugner upset by Bodell

After losing the British title to Henry Cooper, Jack Bodell boxed on, winning his next four bouts in a row, and was rewarded for his efforts with a shot at the then-reigning British, European and Commonwealth heavyweight champion, Joe Bugner.

The contest took place on 27th September 1971, at the Empire Pool, Wembley, London. Bugner was the firm favourite to retain the titles. After all, Bugner had defeated Henry Cooper, the man who had beaten Bodell twice.

Surely the outcome was obvious to all who follow the sport. Bodell didn't read the script – he didn't come to lose. He threw the kitchen sink at Bugner and stormed to a fifteen round points victory. The former British champion was a revelation in the contest. This was a stunning result, which confounded the critics. Many now started to revalue the ability of Bodell, and felt he might just be able to produce more outstanding victories. That was not so.

In his next fight after defeating Bugner, he stepped in with highly-ranked Jerry Quarry on 16th November 1971. The meeting with the American frankly looked to be very ambitious. Many viewed this fight with trepidation, fearing the worst for him. The venue for the Bodell-Quarry fight was once again the Empire Pool. As generally expected, Quarry was just too much for Bodell, knocking him out in the first round of ten. Quarry must have felt that Christmas had come early for him, such was the ease of his victory.

After the Quarry disaster, it was all downhill from that point on for Bodell. He next packed his suitcase and travelled to Spain. It wasn't for a well-deserved rest, far from it. The trip was for business, not pleasure. It was to defend his European crown against former holder José Manuel Urtain, on 17th December 1971.

The fight took place at the Palacio de los Deportes. The

British fighter lost the title when stopped in the second stanza of fifteen. Bodell next saw action on 27th June 1972, at Villa Park. Birmingham, West Midlands, against Northern Ireland's Danny McAlinden. Once again, Bodell crashed to defeat when his challenger knocked him out in round two of fifteen, which saw him lose the British and Commonwealth heavyweight titles to McAlinden.

Bodell's Final Contest

The defeat against Danny McAlinden, when defending his British and Commonwealth heavyweight titles, was the last time that Jack Bodell would step inside the ring to do battle. His time in the sport was over. He later decided to retire from boxing. He left the sport with a professional record of seventy-one bouts, winning fifty-eight, and losing thirteen.

Chapter Fifteen
Cooper Defeats Urtain

José Manuel Urtain

The Spaniard José Manuel Urtain was the next man for Henry Cooper to share the ring with. He was the current European heavyweight champion – a title which Cooper had set his sights on regaining.

In the early stages of his career, Urtain looked to be a genuine prospect in the division, a threat to the other contenders. He was disposing of his opponents with relative ease, stopping them well before the final bell. His punching power was being noticed by several fight aficionados, who could see good things for him in the months to come. There was talk of him being given a shot at the world title should he continue winning. He was even attracting attention in the USA, which takes some doing.

Urtain had won the European crown on 3rd April 1970, when he knocked out holder Peter Weiland of Germany, in round seven of fifteen, at the Palacio de los Deportes, Madrid, Comunidad de Madrid, Spain. Urtain made the first defence of the crown on 22nd June 1970, when he outpointed Germany's Jurgen Blin over fifteen rounds at the Plaza de Toros Monumental, Barcelona, Cataluna, Spain. Urtain, while not a fancy-dan boxing-wise, was a strong fighter who would engage in close combat with his opponents when in the ring. He also appeared to be very durable, which is a big plus when exchanging punches with the big boys in the division.

Going into the bout with Cooper, Urtain had a slate of thirty-two bouts, winning thirty-one, with one defeat. The loss came at the hands of Italian Alfredo Vogrig on 1st August 1970, by way of a disqualification in round three of ten, in a bout that had taken place at the Plazza de Toros del Chofre, San Sebastian, Pais, Vasco, Spain. It was deemed that during the bout, Urtain had landed a low blow, which incapacitated Vogrig. In his last contest before meeting Cooper, Urtain had boxed on 2nd October 1970, stopping Stamford Harris in round two of ten. The venue for the Urtain-Harris bout was Frankfurt, Hessen, Germany.

On close inspection of Urtain's record, it was noticeable that he had not fought anyone near world-class during his time in the sport. It was always possible that Urtain might come of age on the night and overcome Cooper's vast experience to prove he was the real deal. Urtain was a tough *hombre* – of that there was not a shadow of a doubt. Any rough inside work would suit the robust champion, with the possible outcome of Cooper being badly cut around the eyes, and hence see him defeated.

Cooper, as always, entered the ring at the Empire Pool, Wembley, London, with the spectators strongly behind him, chanting his name repeatedly. Cooper was now more than a fighter to British fans – he had become the bedrock of the sport in the UK, a hero to the many who followed boxing. The defending champion looked a little apprehensive in his corner while waiting for the bout to commence. He and his corner team were fully aware that Cooper represented the sternest test yet in the Spaniard's career. A loss here for Urtain would shatter any future dreams of glory he might have harboured. A defeat would see him go back to square one, having to rebuild his career. The tension in the arena was at an all-time high, even before the bell rang out to start the battle. It was heart-thumping stuff. It was a contest which would decide who the best heavyweight in Europe was, with the added lure of high-profile fights in the pipeline for the victor.

When the fight started, Cooper looked for the opening in his opponent's defence and fired a left jab into his face. The champion attempted to avoid the blow by moving his head side to side. The action was quickly heating up. Both men were looking to dominate their opponent and take an early lead. The two fighters occasionally fell into a clinch, which, for a moment, slowed the pace. When the two boxers stepped away from each other, Cooper was seen to be cut over the left eye. It looked to be a bad wound: not a great start for the challenger. He still had a long way to go in the fight. He had been on this injury path many times before. It wasn't a path he would have chosen by choice, but here he was, and he now had to cope with the situation.

To his credit, Cooper didn't show any signs of distress. He was the consummate professional, boxing in a cool manner. He went back to his corner looking unperturbed when the round ended. Cooper's team, on the other hand, looked a little worried as they went about the task of patching up the wound to stop the blood flow.

Urtain, at this point, would have been somewhat happy about Cooper's injury and may well have thought he was on his way to a certain victory. A solid punch to the wound would open the cut even further, most certainly bringing the bout to a premature end. A victory for Urtain would, without doubt, be the best of his career. Such a win would put him well and truly on the international map, with his services being much in demand.

In the second session, Cooper started sharply shooting out his left hand into the Spaniard's face. The champion, true to his reputation, was strong – he pushed forward, catching Cooper with his own jab, which had some force behind it. He knew he had to hurt the champion to instil a degree of hesitancy into his work and stop him advancing towards him. At the same time, Cooper had to protect his eye; the damaged, bloody flesh around the wound continued to be an ever-inviting target for the champion. Urtain bullied Cooper against the ropes, throwing what looked like, at first sight, clumsy punches, but that was a misnomer; the punches had some sting in them. The fight was not easy for Cooper, who knew he was walking a tightrope each second the fight lasted. Another punch on the cut would cause even more damage, encouraging the blood to flow with more intensity. Should this happen, the referee would have no choice but to step in and stop the bout.

When the stanza ended, Cooper strolled back to his corner, looking somewhat relieved that he had survived the session without getting any further damage to the cut.

However, he was not out of the woods yet – not by a

long way. Urtain had proved to be a tough opponent, tougher than many had expected prior to his meeting with Cooper. He may have been showing a lack of boxing ability, but he was a strong man who was giving Cooper a hard fight.

In rounds three and four, Cooper took command with his better boxing, which gave the sense that he was on his way to victory.

However, in the fifth session, Cooper suffered another cut under the right eye, which put his chance of regaining the European crown in jeopardy. The damage to Cooper's optics would encourage Urtain to increase his efforts even further to defeat the man standing in front of him. When a bloody Cooper returned to his corner after the stanza was completed, there was a feeling of dread amongst the spectators. They hoped for the best, but feared that the cuts would determine the outcome of the fight. The challenger was up against it, and he needed to put an end to the contest as quickly as possible.

In the sixth session, Cooper brought his vast ring experience into play. He was now beginning to judge the distance better than before, scoring with his classic jab, which pushed Urtain's head back, sending out a spray of sweat and blood into the air. There was still some way to go yet, but Cooper was clearly in the ascendancy at this stage of the melee. He was looking good, looking composed. He just had to ensure that he protected the cuts around his eyes, which was no easy task. Urtain was a brave fighter – no one could take that fact away from him. He was taking heavy punishment, but still pushed forward, ignoring the pain he must have been feeling from the punches he was receiving from Cooper. Needless to say, they were not love taps. The spectators felt that Cooper was now well and truly on his way to victory. He just had to box clever, be patient and not take any unnecessary chances. He needed to refrain from getting drawn into any close encounter exchanges. This would play into Urtain's hands, since there would be every possibility that their heads might clash, and Cooper's cuts might worsen. The champion continued to walk forward like a tank with no reverse gear, still looking to find a way to defeat his challenger. There was no quit in the man. Urtain was a proud fighter, but he must have now realised, deep down, that his hopes of returning to Spain with the title firmly within his grasp was unlikely. Cooper had been around the sport long enough to know that he could not ease off. He still had a job to do and continued to dish out the punishment on his opponent, who was now looking more than a little battle weary.

The end came in round eight, when the referee decided that Urtain had taken more than enough and decided it was time to call a halt to the contest. Their decision to stop the fight was a wise one, under the circumstances. The contest had become very much a one-sided affair, with the Spanish fighter taking punch after punch to both head and body. Urtain would return to Spain as an ex-title holder. He had fallen short against the British fighter. In defeat, he had shown great courage and had nothing to be ashamed of. He went out like a true champion. Cooper confirmed, in defeating Urtain, that he was the top fighter in Europe, with his eyes firmly set on lucrative defences in the months to follow. He may not have been in the first flush of youth, but he was still a force to be reckoned with. He was not yet ready for a rocking chair and slippers.

Three Times a Champion

When Henry Cooper defeated José Manuel Urtain to win the European heavyweight championship, he achieved the feat of becoming the first boxer in the weight division to have won the EBU title on three separate occasions. That was quite an accomplishment.

The European Boxing Union

Before being renamed the EBU, the organisation was known as the IBU. They duly controlled European title fights before 1946. The first fighter to capture the EBU heavyweight title was Bruce Woodcock of the UK, who won the vacant crown, knocking out Albert Renet of France in round six of fifteen. The contest was staged at Kings Hall, Belle Vue, Manchester, Lancashire, on 29th July 1946.

Champion Once Again

After losing his European heavyweight title to Henry Cooper, it looked as if José Manuel Urtain's moment in the big time had come and gone.

To his credit, he fought on, duly challenging for the European championship seven fights later, and hence regained the crown on 17th December 1971. Urtain took the European title from the then reigning champion, Jack Bodell. The Urtain-Bodell fight took place at the Palacio de los Deportes, Madrid, Comunidad, de Madrid, Spain. Urtain looked sharp – he was really on his game and won by way of a stoppage in round two of fifteen. Urtain had lost the title to one Briton and regained it from another British fighter in the shape of Bodell. This must have given him great satisfaction. There was no getting away from the fact that Urtain looked good in his winning contest against Bodell. It appeared that he may get involved in bigger fights down the line. However, any hope of bigger fights for Urtain quickly disappeared. His reign as European champion was short-lived.

In his first defence, Urtain was defeated by Jurgen Blin of Germany on 9th June 1972, when he was outpointed over fifteen rounds. The venue for the Blin-Urtain contest was the Palacio de Deportes, de la Comunidad, de Madrid, Spain.

Despite this defeat, Urtain did not give up on his fistic career. He still had ambitions and hoped that he might still be able to climb back to championship status. Urtain once again attempted to become European heavyweight champion when he contested the then vacant crown on 12th March 1977. He travelled to Belgium to meet home fighter Jean-Pierre Coopman at the Sportpaleis, Anterwerpen, whereupon he met with defeat, when knocked out in round four of fifteen.

José Manuel Urtain's Farewell to Boxing

The contest for the vacant European heavyweight title against Jean-Pierre Coopman was José Manuel Urtain's final foray in the professional ring. He later retired from boxing with a professional record of sixty-eight bouts, of which he won fifty-three, losing eleven, with four drawn. During his time in boxing, Urtain brought a degree of excitement to the sport.

Chapter Sixteen
Cooper Retires from Boxing

Joe Bugner

Joe Bugner was the new exciting hope in the British ranks – a fighter from whom great things were expected. His big chance came when he stepped up to challenge Henry Cooper for the British, European and Commonwealth titles on 16th March 1971, at the Empire Pool, Wembley, London. Bugner had a good resumé of thirty-four bouts, which saw him win thirty-one, with two defeats, and one draw.

In his last bout before meeting Cooper, Bugner had not exactly given an inspiring performance against opponent Bill Drover of Canada, at York Hall, Bethnal Green, London, on 10th February 1971. The contest went the full distance of ten rounds and resulted in a draw. This was a disappointing performance from Bugner. He was expected to glide past Drover with comparative ease. It was hardly a confidence builder for him, going into a title fight against a man of Cooper's class.

Despite that dismal result, it was felt that Bugner, with youth on his side at the age of twenty-one years and three days, might very well take the titles from Cooper, who was aged thirty-six years, ten months, and thirteen days, with a long career behind him. Cooper had a number of miles on the clock. It was likely that Bugner could be in the right place at the right time. The champion had been the top man in the UK for a considerable period of time. However, saying that, it was one of those fights where you could present an argument for either man winning on the night.

Many hoped that Cooper would remain on top of the tree; he had been good for British boxing and had given the game many exciting moments. Sentiment dictated that Cooper would continue to dominate the UK scene and turn back Bugner, like he had so many challengers in the past. Yet it was apparent that Cooper's time was coming to an end – the sands of time were fast running out for him. Let's make no bones about it – boxing is a hard and relentless sport which, over a period of time, takes its toll on the body. The training in the gym becomes tougher, the road work more demanding. The life of a boxer is a tough one; it doesn't get any easier with the onset of age.

Going into the Bugner fight, Cooper had been boxing in the professional ranks for sixteen years, six months and two days. That's a very long time for anyone involved in the sport of pugilism. Bugner had obviously not boxed as long as Cooper, but he had served a good apprenticeship leading up to this moment. He had faced fighters of various styles along the way, preparing for this occasion.

Bugner had made his debut in the paid ranks on 20th December 1967, at the Hilton Hotel, Mayfair, London. It wasn't the best of starts for the young boxer. In fact, it was a disaster. His opponent, Paul Brown, knocked him out in round three of six. Bugner recovered from this setback and worked his way into contention. Bugner's manager, Andy Smith, was confident that his charge was ready to take the titles from Cooper. The contest drew a great deal of attention from both the media and the public at large. It was a major talking point in the UK. Whenever Cooper fought, it was newsworthy; it was good copy for the sports pages of the various newspapers and magazines. It was an event.

When the moment of the fight arrived, the two boxers faced each other in the ring, listening to the final instructions of the referee in charge of the contest. Both champion and challenger looked intense. There was, after all, a great deal riding on the fight.

Once the bell sounded to start the hostilities, the two men met in the centre of the ring and studied each other for a moment. Then Bugner went to work, shooting out a left jab into the champion's face. Cooper retaliated with a solid jab of his own, which jolted Bugner's head back on his shoulders. The fight was already starting to get interesting.

In the second stanza, the bout followed a similar fashion, with both champion and challenger snaking out their left jabs to the face, occasionally changing tactics, landing solid blows to the body. As always, there was the fear that Cooper could get cut while exchanging punches with Bugner. The champion was constantly looking to land his left hook on his challenger. Should he connect, it could well bring the contest to a close, but could he land it? That was the big question. Bugner was agile and had shown a good defence. He was not shipping any damaging blows. By this time, Cooper had realised that Bugner had more boxing *nous* than his previous opponent José Manuel Urtain, and was proving to be a difficult proposition. Cooper could not relax for a minute – he had to stay focused every second of the round.

In the third stanza, Cooper sustained a cut over his left eyebrow, which brought a slight frown from his fans. The wound must have given Bugner hope that he just might be able to end the fight before the final round was reached. Yet this wound was something Cooper had more than learned to live with during his long career in the ring.

At the end of the session, the champion's cut was treated expertly in the corner. When the bell tolled to start the next stanza, a very determined Cooper took the fight to his challenger, looking to land a series of crisp punches on his opponent. Bugner showed his boxing skills, by avoiding a number of the shots coming his way.

In the rounds which followed, the two fighters engaged in a technical battle, each man attempting to out-think the other.

Then in the seventh stanza, Cooper picked up another cut this time under his right eye. This was not good. He really didn't need more facial damage. Things were not going entirely in the champion's favour. He had to fight hard for every point earned. Bugner was acquitting himself well against the champion, showing durability complemented by good boxing skills. This version of Bugner was far better than the one who had fought Bill Drover in his previous bout. The tension was building, and the fighters were turning up the heat on each other. The fight was developing into an absorbing encounter.

It was neck and neck going into the eighth session, with the feeling that the contest could go either way. Both men knew the fight was close – they needed to dig deep.

In the later stages of the contest, Cooper looked to be taking the lead, attacking a back-pedalling Bugner. The champion was still looking to land his left hook, but the challenger was having none of it. He would often block the punch with an effective guard. It was apparent that Cooper was not going to halt Bugner, and he would need to go the full distance to achieve a victory.

The rounds slipped by, and each stanza showcased the left jabs of both fighters.

The final round arrived, which saw both champion and challenger put in a massive effort to secure a victory.

When the bell sounded to end the bout, many felt that Cooper had done enough to retain his titles, but that was not so – the decision was given to Bugner. The verdict was greeted with a chorus of booing from the spectators. Cooper had lost his three titles to Bugner by a quarter of a point – a fact which many found hard to accept. Yet the decision was made, and the now ex-champion left the ring for the last time. He made his way to the dressing room, where he announced his retirement from the sport. It was the end of an era, one which had seen Cooper reign supreme over the domestic heavyweight scene for many years with a grip of iron. When you thought of the British heavyweight title, you immediately thought of Henry Cooper. It seemed hard to believe that Cooper would never again enter the fray to box, but he had made a wise and sensible decision. Many fighters go on too long, losing to opponents whom they would have beaten easily in their prime. Cooper would not go down that road; he was not going to be a stepping stone for other fighters on their way up. He left boxing at the right time with his reputation fully intact.

Cooper's Resumé

Henry Cooper retired from boxing with a resumé of fifty-five contests, which consisted of forty wins, fourteen defeats, with one draw.

In the Opposite Corner

Danny Holland, throughout much of Henry Cooper's career, had served in his corner as a cuts man. In this capacity, he had been of great assistance to Cooper, showing his vast expertise in helping to stem the flow of blood from any cuts he may have sustained during the heat of battle. This time around, Holland was in the corner of Joe Bugner.

On His Own Terms

It is a shame that Henry Cooper was unable to leave boxing with a win in his last contest. It would have been a fitting finale to his career had he been able to do so. Yet, it has to be said that even with the defeat to Joe Bugner, Cooper walked away from the sport on his own terms, with his head held high. That is something many fighters have failed to do in the past.

No Return with Bugner

Often, when a champion loses his titles by a close points decision, which is deemed as being controversial, a return between the two fighters is often arranged. However, Henry Cooper was adamant that he had retired, and there would be no return to face Joe Bugner.

No Comeback

Sadly, many boxers who have retired from the sport have often been tempted to return to the ring after a period of time for various reasons. Former champions and non-champions have unwisely pulled on the gloves to give it one more try, feeling that they still had something left to offer and had a couple of good fights left inside them.

More often than not, they find that the return was ill-advised and they end their career being defeated by opponents who would have not have laid a glove on them in their peak days. It was pleasing that Henry Cooper did not contemplate a comeback at a later date, and fall into that trap. He was aware that his time fighting was over, and found other outlets to keep himself occupied, and in doing so, he kept his legacy intact.

The Last Referee

Harry Gibbs officiated at the Henry Cooper-Joe Bugner British, European and Commonwealth heavyweight title bout. In so doing, he became the last man to referee a contest which involved Cooper.

The Last Promoter

Harry Levene staged the Henry Cooper-Joe Bugner British, European, and Commonwealth heavyweight championship bout. This meant that Levene became the last promoter to stage a contest which involved Cooper.

The New Champion

Frankly, Joe Bugner's victory over Henry Cooper did not sit well with many followers of boxing, who felt that the defending champion deserved to get the victory.

On the other hand, there were those who felt Bugner did just enough to get the decision and would inject new life into the domestic division. Nevertheless, whatever the views held about Bugner, he was the new British, European and Commonwealth heavyweight champion, and it looked as if the world was now his oyster. It would be true to say that Bugner had his share of ups and downs in the years which followed.

After the Cooper victory, he made the first defence of the European heavyweight title against Germany's Jurgen Blin on 11th May 1971, at the Empire Pool, Wembley, London, and retained the crown by way of a fifteen-round points decision. While victorious, Bugner didn't exactly set the world on fire with his performance.

Then, against all expectations, in his next outing on 27th September 1971, at the Empire Pool, he lost the British, European and Commonwealth titles to Jack Bodell, when it went down to a fifteen-round points decision. This was disappointing, but Bugner overcame this defeat and went on to have a good career, which saw him meet some of the best heavyweights in the world.

On 14th February 1973, Bugner ventured to the Convention Center, Las Vegas, Nevada, USA, to engage Muhammad Ali in a twelve-round contest. At that time, Ali was a former world heavyweight champion. The contest went the full distance, which saw Bugner lose on a points decision.

On 2nd July 1973, Bugner met another former world

heavyweight king in the shape of Joe Frazier at Earls Court Arena, Kensington, London. Once again, the contest was scheduled for twelve rounds, of which Frazier emerged the victor, giving Bugner his second defeat in succession. While losing to Frazier, Bugner gave a performance which drew praise from many critics. A world title chance came around for Bugner on 30th June 1975 against Muhammad Ali, who had since regained the undisputed world heavyweight title from George Foreman by a knockout in round eight of fifteen.

The contest took place at the Stade du 20 Mai, Kinshasa, Democratic Republic of the Congo, on 30th October 1974. The venue for the Ali-Bugner contest was Merdeka Stadium, Kula Lumpur, Malaysia. After fifteen rounds, Bugner was declared the loser when Ali retained the championship on points.

During his boxing career, Bugner won the British and Commonwealth heavyweight crown twice and the European title three times, which was impressive. He also won the lightly-regarded WBF world heavyweight title on 4th July 1998, when he defeated former WBA world heavyweight king James Smith, who retired in the first stanza of a scheduled twelve. The venue for this contest was the Carrara Basketball Stadium, Queensland, Australia.

Bugner's Last Appearance in the Ring

After his victory over Henry Cooper, Joe Bugner took part in a further forty-eight bouts of which he won thirty-seven and lost eleven. His last appearance in a professional ring took place on 13th June 1999, against American Levi Billups. Bugner won by a disqualification in the ninth stanza of ten.

The venue for the contest was Jupiter's Hotel & Casino, Broadbeach, Queensland, Australia. During his career, Bugner participated in eighty-three bouts, consisting of sixty-nine victories with thirteen defeats, and one draw.

More British Title Contests

Henry Cooper retired from boxing, holding the record of competing in more British heavyweight title bouts than any previous boxer. The total held was twelve, of which he won ten.

Opponents in Common

In the professional ranks, Henry Cooper and Muhammad Ali had six opponents in common:

Joe Bugner
Zora Folley
Brian London
Karl Mildenberger
Alex Miteff
Floyd Patterson

More Commonwealth Title Contests

Henry Cooper holds the record of competing in more Commonwealth heavyweight title contests than any other boxer at the time he retired from the sport. He had taken part in thirteen bouts, of which he won eleven.

Inside the Distance Victories

During his reign as British and Commonwealth heavyweight champion, Henry Cooper won eight of his title fights inside the scheduled distance. This was more than any other previous holder of these titles had achieved during their respective times as champion.

Venues

Henry Cooper boxed at various venues during his professional career. See below for the number of times Cooper boxed at each venue.

Venues are presented in alphabetical order.

Arsenal Stadium	Once
Coney Beach, Pleasure Park	Twice
De Montfort Hall	Once
Earl's Court Arena	Five
Empire Pool	Fifteen
Empress Hall	Once
Festfalenhallen	Once
Harringay Arena	Seven
Ice Rink, Nottingham	Twice
Johanneshovs Ice Stadium	Once
Kings Hall, Belle Vue	Three
London Olympia	Once
Manor Place Baths	Twice
Molineux Stadium	Once
PalaEur	Once
Royal Albert Hall	Four
St. Andrews (Birmingham)	Once
Wembley Stadium	Once
Westfalenhallen	Twice
White City Stadium	Once
Wolverhampton Civic Hall	Twice

Boxing Abroad

During his professional boxing career, Henry Cooper boxed abroad on five occasions:

Sweden	Once
Germany	Three times
Italy	Once

Eight European Champions

While being a European heavyweight champion during his professional career, Henry Cooper also fought eight opponents who had either held, or went on to win, the European crown, be it at heavy or light-heavyweight.

See below in alphabetical order:

Jack Bodell
Joe Bugner
Ingemar Johannson
Karl Mildenberger
Heinz Neuhaus
Dick Richardson
Erich Shoppner (light-heavyweight)
José Manuel Urtain

European Heavyweight Title Bouts

During his time in the professional ranks, Henry Cooper participated in six bouts, which involved the European heavyweight title. Cooper won four and lost two of said bouts.

Fought Three World Champions

While boxing in the professional ranks, Henry Cooper crossed gloves with three fighters who held, or were former, world heavyweight champions.

See below in alphabetical order:

Muhammad Ali
Ingemar Johannson
Floyd Patterson

Five World Title Challengers

During his time in the professional ranks, Henry Cooper shared the ring with five fighters who had challenged, and failed to win, the world heavyweight title.

See below in alphabetical order:

Joe Bugner
Zora Folley
Roy Harris
Brian London
Karl Mildenberger

British Title Holders

Henry Cooper shared the ring during his professional career with four opponents who had, at one time or another, held the British heavyweight title.

See across the page in alphabetical order:

Jack Bodell
Joe Bugner
Joe Erskine
Brian London

Commonwealth title holders

Henry Cooper fought five opponents during his professional career, who had, at one time or another, held the Commonwealth title.

See below in alphabetical order:

Jack Bodell
Joe Bugner
Joe Bygraves
Joe Erskine
Brian London

More Than Once

Henry Cooper fought the listed boxers more than once in the professional ranks.

See below in alphabetical order:

Muhammad Ali	Twice
Uber Bacilieri	Twice
Jack Bodell	Twice
Joe Bygraves	Twice
Joe Erskine	Five times
Brian London	Three times
Dick Richardson	Twice

Undefeated Fighters

Henry Cooper fought five boxers in the professional ranks who were undefeated at the time of his meeting with them.

See below in alphabetical order:

Muhammad Ali
Joe Erskine
Ingemar Johannson
Brian London
Erich Schoppner

Various Countries

During his time in the professional ranks, Henry Cooper met a number of boxers who were born outside of the UK.

See below in alphabetical order:

America	Thirteen
Argentina	One
France	One
Germany	Four
Italy	Three
Jamaica	One
South Africa	Two
Spain	One
Sweden	One

(While Joe Bugner was born in Hungary, he was a British boxer when he boxed Henry Cooper.)

Bates Only British Born Boxer

Only one British-born heavyweight boxer stopped Henry Cooper inside the scheduled distance in the professional ranks. That was Peter Bates, who, on 7th September 1956, accomplished this feat at the Kings Hall, Belle Vue, Manchester, Lancashire. Bates stopped Cooper in round five of ten due to a cut eye injury.

The Oldest Man

The oldest man to challenge Henry Cooper for the British and Commonwealth heavyweight titles was former champion Joe Erskine, who failed to regain the titles on 2nd April 1962, when the fight was stopped in round nine of fifteen. At the time of the contest, Erskine was twenty-eight years, two months and seven days old. The Cooper-Erskine bout took place at the Ice Rink, Nottingham, Nottinghamshire.

Fastest Victory in a Title Contest

Henry Cooper secured his fastest victory in a title contest on 13th June 1967, when defending his British and Commonwealth heavyweight titles. He stopped Jack Bodell in round two of fifteen. The bout took place at Molineux Grounds, Wolverhampton, West Midlands.

Olympic Gold Medallist

Henry Cooper boxed two men in the professional ranks who, during their amateur careers, won gold medals at the Olympic Games. Cassius Clay, at light-heavyweight, took the top prize in the tournament, which took place in Rome, Italy (1960), out-pointing Zbigniew Pietrzykowsi of Poland over three rounds. Floyd Patterson won gold in the middleweight division at the games, which took place in Helsinki, Finland (1952), knocking out opponent Vasile Tita of Romania in the first round of three.

Chapter Seventeen

Life After Boxing

An Audience with Muhammad Ali

Henry Cooper appeared on the TV show *An Audience with Muhammad Ali* on 27th December 1974. This must have rekindled many old memories for both Cooper and Ali. The programme was hosted by Dickie Davies, in a good-humoured and entertaining way. The show was a treat for boxing fans.

When introduced, Ali entered the set dressed smartly, with a black stylish walking cane. The audience consisted of various celebrities which included Reg Gutteridge (boxing journalist) Beryl Cameron-Gibbons (boxing promoter), Len Harvey (who during his boxing career had held a number of impressive titles such as the British and Commonwealth middleweight, British and Commonwealth light-heavyweight), and British and Commonwealth heavyweight crowns, Colin Hart (boxing journalist), Julie Welch (journalist), Frank McGhee (journalist), Alan Hubbard (journalist), Ken Jones (journalist), John Alderton (actor), Ed Stewart (radio and TV presenter), Terry Mancini (footballer), Billy Knight (boxer), and Neil Durden-Smith (radio and TV sports presenter).

Ali was never on the ropes and pulled no punches when answering the many questions put to him in a light-hearted and very comical way. Ali even took the time to give some boxing tips to Isaac Fleming, a young boxer in the audience. To use boxing terminology, the show was a knockout.

The Joe Bromley Award

In 1975, Henry Cooper was presented with The Joe Bromley Award, which is recognition given by the Boxing Writer's Club for outstanding services to the sport of boxing. Cooper was the eighth boxer to have received this award.

See the list below:

Len Harvey	1967
Larry Gains	1968
Chris Finnegan	1969
Jack Petersen	1970
Ken Buchanan	1971
Teddy Waltham	1972
Terry Waller:	1974

(Note: there was no award presented in 1973.)

Cooper the Actor

Many boxers over the years have turned their hand to acting. Henry Cooper was no exception to the rule. He played the role of prize fighter John Gully, who later became a Member of Parliament in the 1975 film, *Royal Flash*. The film was directed by Richard Lester, and produced by Denis O'Dell and David V. Picker. It starred Malcolm McDowell, Oliver

Reed, Alan Bates and Florinda Bolkan. While Cooper was not going to be another Sir Laurence Oliver, he put in a more than passable acting performance in the production.

John Gully

John Gully, who was portrayed by Henry Cooper in the film *Royal Flash*, was a very interesting character. He was born on 21st August 1783. Gully was released from debtors' prison and became a successful prize fighter. He was not only handy with his fists; he also became a very successful horse breeder. It didn't stop there. Gully later became a member of parliament for Pontefract Constituency from December 1832-1837. He died on 9th March 1863.

Cooper the Singer

During 1976, Henry Cooper turned his attention to singing and released a record called 'Knock Me Down with a Feather'. To his credit, Cooper gave a good rendition of a happy-go-lucky song, which was composed by Rick Cassman.

Papal Knighthood

In 1978, yet another honour came Henry Cooper's way, when he was awarded the Papal Knighthood. This was a well-deserved award for Cooper for his services to a number of charities over the years.

Muhammad Ali This is Your Life

In December 1978, Henry Cooper paid homage to his former rival, three-time world heavyweight champion, Muhammad Ali who was the subject of the TV show, *This is Your Life*. Ali had no idea what he was walking into when he entered the studio, and was greeted with great applause from those in attendance. The shock and surprise on Ali's face was clear to see.

The programme was introduced by Eamonn Andrews. The show looked back on Ali's life, and all those whom he had come into contact with, and had made an impact on him and his career over the years.

Cooper of course, recalled his meetings in the ring with the great champion. Apart from Cooper, a number of guests appeared on the show, including Ali's then wife, Veronica, along with his parents, Odessa and Cassius Clay Snr, Rahaman Ali (Ali's brother), Tom Jones (singer), Jimmy Ellis (former WBA world heavyweight title holder), Ronnie O'Keefe (Ali's first amateur opponent), Joe E. Martin (who introduced Ali to boxing), Fred Stoner (trainer), Angelo Dundee (Ali's professional trainer), Zbigniew Pietrzykowski (who fought Ali in the Olympic games final), Wilma Rudolph (a sprinter who won three gold medals at the Rome Olympic Games), Drew Bundini Brown, and his assistant trainer, Howard Bingham (a friend and a renowned photographer). Also the former undisputed world heavyweight king Joe Frazier (who fought Ali in three exciting bouts, etched into the memories of fight fans the world over). The show was well received and gave an interesting insight to the great champion.

The Plank

Henry Cooper appeared as a man drinking in a pub in the TV version of *The Plank* in 1979. The comedy film had a mixture of personalities from the entertainment world, including Eric Sykes, Arthur Lowe, Lionel Blair, Harry H. Corbett, Bernard Cribbins, Robert Dorning, Diana Dors,

Charlie Drake, Jimmy Edwards, Liza Goddard, Deryck Guyler, Charles Hawtrey, Frankie Howerd, James Hunt, Wilfred Hyde-White, Joanna Lumley, Kenny Lynch, Brian Murphy, Kate O'Mara, Ann Sidney, Reg Varney and Frank Windsor.

Rocky Balboa Meets Henry Cooper

Both boxing and film fans alike were given a special treat on the 17th July 1982. Sylvester Stallone and Henry Cooper were interviewed by Gloria Hunniford on the BBC One *Saturday Live* show. Stallone spoke about his then latest film, *Rocky III*. During the course of the programme, he also discussed the sport of boxing with Cooper.

Golden Belt

A new boxing series hit the TV screens in 1983, entitled, *Henry Cooper's Golden Belt.* The format of the show was to pit amateur clubs against each other in an inter-city challenge, the ultimate prize being the titular £1000 belt. Cooper would often chat with the young boxers who were competing, along with their parents. Guest boxers who had attained world champion status during professional their careers like Alan Minter (middleweight), Charlie Magri (flyweight), Maurice Hope (super-welterweight), and John H. Stracey (welterweight), made appearances on the programme. There was always the chance that viewers would see a future champion in action. Dave Brenner gave the commentary on the contests.

The State of Boxing

On 11th Februay1990, a massive upset took place which shook the foundations world of boxing. Mike Tyson lost his WBC, WBA and IBF world heavyweight titles to James Buster Douglas at The Tokyo Dome, Tokyo, Japan. The defeat of Tyson was not predicted by anyone in the fight game. The loss came by way of a ten round knockout, in a contest scheduled for twelve. The fight and the money involved in the contest was discussed in great detail on the BBC programme, *Newsnight*, which was hosted by Jeremy Paxman. Henry Cooper, along with boxing journalist Reg Gutteridge, gave their expert views on the fight and the current state of boxing. They also discussed the heavyweight contenders in action at that time, and the money involved in the sport.

Gotcha Oscar

Over the years, Henry Cooper had won many awards, and he won yet another on 23rd November 1991. Cooper appeared on the Saturday night BBC TV show, *Noel's House Party*, which was hosted by Noel Edmonds. There was a regular segment in the programme called 'Gotcha', whereupon various celebrities had a practical joke played on them. Cooper became one of the said victims.

He was told that he was filming a documentary on golf, which he was more than pleased to take part in, having a great love for the sport. He was joined on the fairway by the show's co-presenter, the late Keith Chegwin, who posed as part of the documentary team. One frustrating setback after another hindered Cooper's attempts to complete the filming. His patience was tested to the full.

Cooper showed great restraint throughout, revealing that he had a great professionalism and sense of humour. He received the 'Gotcha Oscar' award at the end of what was a very enjoyable show.

Chapter Eighteen

The World Says Goodbye to Henry Cooper

Sold the Belts

Henry Cooper sold all three of his Lonsdale belts for a reported £42,000, after losing heavily on the Lloyds Insurance Market. One of the belts – the last one made of gold – was sold for a reported £22,000. The others sold for £10,000 each. Cooper was expecting £70,000 from the sale, but gained a degree of contentment when they were all sold together. This was a hard knock for Cooper, who had worked hard to win the belts during his time in the ring. It was sad to see him lose the belts in this way.

A Special Award

In 2000, Henry Cooper received the Special Award. This is an award presented by the British Boxing Board of Control to those involved in the sport in one capacity or another, for their respected services to boxing.

Previous recipients of the award:

Dr Adrian Whiteson	1984
Harry Gibbs	1985
Ray Clarke	1986
Hon. Colin Moynihan	1987
Tom Powell	1988
Winston Burnett	1989
Frank Bruno	1990
Muhammad Ali	1991
Doctor Oswald Ross	1992
Phil Martin	1993
Ron Oliver	1994
Gary Davidson	1995
Reg Gutteridge & Harry Carpenter	1996
Miguel Mathews and Pete Buckley	1997
Mickey Duff & Tommy Miller	1998
Jim Evans & Jack Lindsey	1999

Arise, Sir Henry Cooper

Henry Cooper received a knighthood in the 2000 New Year honours awards, for his services to boxing. This was a great honour for Cooper, who became the first boxer to be knighted, but also for the sport in general.

Sad Passing

In 2008, Henry Cooper suffered a personal tragedy, when his wife Albina sadly died. Her death was from a reported heart attack. This was a terrible moment for both Cooper and his family. It was a well-known fact that the couple were devoted to each other.

Another Presentation

On 7th May 2009, Henry Cooper was presented with the Lifetime Achievement Award by Brut and the London Ex-Boxer's Association, in recognition of a great sporting career. The presentation was made at the Repton Boxing Club in London.

Cooper's Brother Passes Away

Henry Cooper's brother George sadly died on 11th April 2010, at the age of seventy-five years, eleven months and eight days. He boxed under the name Jim Cooper. While his ring career may not have been as successful as his twin's, he was nevertheless a talented performer in his own right. Like Henry, he often suffered from cuts over his eyes during a contest. He had a resumé of twenty-one bouts, consisting of sixteen victories, fourteen defeats, with one drawn.

Henry Cooper Passes Away

Henry Cooper sadly passed away on 1st May 2011, just two days before his seventy-seventh birthday. Many messages of condolences poured in once his passing was announced to the public.

The Funeral

Henry's funeral took place at Oxted in Surrey. The streets were lined with many mourners who came to pay their respects to the former boxer. A number of personalities from both the world of sport and showbusiness attended to pay tribute and say their final goodbyes to a man who meant so much to them.

A Statue of Sir Henry Cooper

A bronze cast statue of Henry Cooper, which was sculpted by Carl Payne, was duly erected in Bellingham, South East London. Payne was an award-winning sculptor who brought all his excellent skills into play when working on this project. It was an outstanding tribute to one of Britain's best boxers.

The Final Round

After the retirement of Henry Cooper, the UK finally came up with boxers who were able to win a version of the world heavyweight title. They were: Lennox Lewis, Herbie Hide, Frank Bruno, Henry Akinwande, David Haye, Tyson Fury, Anthony Joshua, Daniel Dubois and let's be cheeky, and include Michael Bentt, who lived and fought out of the USA, but was born in the UK. They were all able to acquire the status of world heavyweight champion.

Some might say this makes Cooper's achievements look pale in comparison to the aforementioned fighters. However, it shouldn't be forgotten that Cooper fought when things were a little different from the way they are now. When Cooper fought in title fights, they took place over the duration of fifteen rounds, but now they are staged over twelve. The heavyweights are now taller and much heavier than they previously were when Cooper was fighting. It should also be remembered that when Cooper was throwing leather inside the ring, there were only two major world boxing organisations who recognised world title bouts; the WBC and the WBA. There are now four, with the addition of the IBF and WBO, who also recognise world title bouts, plus a number of minor organisations.

One could say it now makes it that much easier to obtain a world title in this era than it was in Cooper's time. That's not to demean the present fighters, who have won a championship; it still takes hard work and dedication to do so. The question being: had there been four options in Cooper's day, as there are now, would he have been able to win a version of the title? It is a tantalising question.

Sadly, I think the answer would have to be a resounding no. Muhammad Ali would have reigned supreme and gathered all the versions of the championship to become the undisputed champion. Even had Ali not been around, there were some really tough nuts to crack at that time. Being king of the world would have been great for Cooper's career but even without the world crown as previously stated, he had an excellent career – one which he could look back on with pride. Many a boxer who's laced on a pair of gloves would have loved to have received the kind of acclaim Cooper had during his stint inside the ring.

As stated earlier in this book, Cooper was a true people's champion. He was a superstar, an icon of his time, a man who was greeted with a great deal of respect by fans wherever he went. Cooper's popularity will not be eclipsed by modern day fighters. He had a magic which will be difficult to be duplicated, even by those who have won a world title.

Henry Cooper's Professional Boxing Record

Abbreviations

W	**Won**
L	**Lost**
PTS	**Points**
KO	**Knockout**
RSF	**Referee Stopped Fight**
RTD	**Retired**
DISQ	**Disqualified**

1954

14th September, Harry Painter. W-KO 1. Harringay Arena, Harringay London.

19th October, Dinny Powell. W-RSF 4. Harringay Arena, Harringay, London.

23rd November. Eddie Keith. W-RSF 1.
Manor Place Baths, Walworth, London.

7th December. Denny Ball W-KO 3.
Harringay Arena, Harringay, London.

1955

27th January. Colin Strauch. W-RSF 1.
Royal Albert Hall, Kensington, London.

8th February. Cliff Purnell. W-PTS 6
Harringay Arena, Harringay, London.

8th March. Hugh Ferns. W-DISQ 2.
Earl's Court Arena, Kensington, London.

29th March. Joe Crickmar. W-RSF 5.
Earl's Court Arena, Kensington, London.

18th April. Joe Bygraves. W-PTS 8.
Manor Place Baths, Walworth, London.

26th April. Uber Bacilieri. L-RSF 2.
Harringay Arena, Harringay, London.

6th June. Ron Harman. W-RSF 7.
Ice Rink, Nottingham, Nottinghamshire.

13th September. Uber Bacilieri. W-KO 7.
White City Stadium, White City, London.

15th November. Joe Erskine. L-PTS 10.
Harringay Arena, Harringay, London.
(Eliminator for British heavyweight title.)

1956
28th February. Maurice Mols. W-RSF 4.
Royal Albert Hall, Kensington, London.

1st May. Brian London. W-RSF 1.
Earl's Court, Empress Hall, Kensington, London.

26th June. Giannino Orlando Luise. W-RSF 7.
Empire Pool, Wembley, London.

7th September. Peter Bates. L-RSF 5.
Kings Hall, Belle Vue, Manchester, Lancashire.

1957
19th February. Joe Bygraves. L-KO 9.
Earl's Court Arena, Kensington, London.
(Challenge for Commonwealth Heavyweight title.)

19th May. Ingemar Johansson. L-KO 5 .
Johanneshovice Ice Stadium, Stockholm, Sweden.
(Challenge for European Heavyweight title.)

17th September. Joe Erskine. L-PTS 15.
Harringay Arena, Harringay, London.
(Challenge for British and Commonwealth Heavyweight titles.)

16th November. Hans Kalbfell. W-PTS 10.
Westfallenhalle, Dortmund, Nordrhein-Westfallen, Germany.

1958

11th January. Heinz Neuhaus DRAW 10.
Westfallenhalle, Dortmund, Nordrhein-Westfallen, Germany.

19th April. Erich Schoppner. L-DISQ 6.
Festhalle, Frankfurt, Hessen, Germany.

3rd September. Dick Richardson. W-RSF 5.
Coney Beach Arena, Porthcawl, Wales.

14th October. Zora Folley. W-PTS 10.
Empire Pool, Wembley, London.

1959

12th January. Brian London. W-PTS 15.
Earl's Court Arena, Kensington, London.
(Challenge for British and Commonwealth heavyweight titles.)

26th August. Gawie de Klerk. W-RSF 5.
Coney Beach Arena, Porthcawl, Wales.
(Defence of Commonwealth heavyweight title.)

17th November. Joe Erskine. W-RSF 12. Earl's Court Arena, Kensington, London.
(Defence of British and Commonwealth heavyweight titles.)

1960

13th September. Roy Harris. W-PTS 10.
Empire Pool, Wembley, London.

6th December. Alex Miteff. W-PTS 10.
Empire Pool, Wembley, London.

1961

21st March. Joe Erskine. W-RSF 5.
Empire Pool, Wembley, London.
(Defence of British and Commonwealth heavyweight titles.)

5th December. Zora Folley. L-KO 2.
Empire Pool, Wembley, London.

1962

23rd January. Tony Hughes. W-RSF 5.
Empire Pool, Wembley, London.

26th February. Wayne Bethea. W-PTS10.
King's Hall, Belle Vue, Manchester, Lancashire.

2nd April. Joe Erskine. W-RSF 9.
Ice Rink, Nottingham, Nottinghamshire.
(Defence of British and Commonwealth heavyweight titles.)

1963

26th March. Dick Richardson. W-KO 5.
Empire Pool, Wembley, London.
(Defence of British and Commonwealth heavyweight titles.)

18th June. Cassius Clay. L-RSF 5.
Wembley Stadium, Wembley, London.
(Cassius Clay later changed his name to Muhammad Ali.)

1964
24th February. Brian London. W-PTS 15.
King's Hall, Belle Vue, Manchester, Lancashire.
(Defence of British and Commonwealth titles plus vacant European Heavyweight crown.)

16th November. Roger Rischer. L-PTS 10.
10 Royal Albert Hall, Kensington, London.

1965
12th January. Dick Wipperman. W-RSF 5.
Royal Albert Hall, Kensington, London.

20th April. Chip Johnson. W-KO 1.
Civic Hall, Wolverhampton, West Midlands.

15th June. Johnny Prescott. W-RTD 10.
St. Andrews (Birmingham City FC), Birmingham.
(Defence of British and Commonwealth heavyweight titles.)

19th October. Amos Johnson. L-PTS 10.
Empire Pool, Wembley, London.

1966
25th January. Hubert Hilton. W-RSF 2.
Olympia, Kensington, London.

16th February. Jefferson Davis. W-KO 1.
Civic Hall, Wolverhampton, West Midlands.

21st May. Muhammad Ali. L-RSF 6.
Arsenal Stadium, Highbury, London.
(Challenge for the WBC world heavyweight title).

20th September. Floyd Patterson. L-KO 4.
Empire Pool, Wembley, London.

1967

17th April. Boston Jacobs. W-PTS 10.
De Montfort Hall, Leicester, Leicestershire.

13th June. Jack Bodell. W-RSF 2.
Molineux Grounds, Wolverhampton, West Midlands.
(Defence of British and Commonwealth heavyweight titles.)

7th November. Billy Walker. W-RSF 6.
Empire Pool, Wembley, London.
(Defence of British and Commonwealth heavyweight titles.)

1968

18th September. Karl Mildenberger. W-DISQ 8.
Empire Pool, Wembley, London.
(Challenge for European Heavyweight title.)

1969

13th March. Piero Tomasoni. W-KO 5.
PalaEur, Roma, Lazio, Italy.
(Defence of European Heavyweight title.)

1970

24th March. Jack Bodell. W-PTS 15.
Empire Pool, Wembley, London.
(Defence of Commonwealth and challenge for British Heavyweight title.)

10th November. José Manuel Urtain. W-RSF 8.
Empire Pool, Wembley, London.
(Challenge for European Heavyweight title.)

1971

16th March. Joe Bugner. L-PTS 15.
Empire Pool, Wembley, London.
(Defence of British, European and Commonwealth Heavyweight titles.)

Bibliography

Books

Cooper, Henry
Henry Cooper's Book of Boxing
Arthur Barker Ltd. 1982

Golesworthy, Maurice
Encyclopaedia of Boxing, 7th Edition
Robert Hale Ltd. 1983

Gutteridge, Reg
The Big Punchers
Stanley Paul 1983

Hugman, Barry J.
British Boxing Yearbook
Newes Books 1985

Roberts, James B. & Skutt, Alexander G.
The Boxing Register
Robson Books Ltd. 1998

Treharne, Evan R.
British Heavyweight Champions
F. C. Avis 1959

Walker, Billy & McGibbon, Robin
When The Gloves Came Off
Robson Books 2007

Magazines

Boxing News 1909 - present.